WHEN THE MILL WHISTLE BLEW

THE WAY IT WAS IN COEUR D'ALENE COUNTRY, 1888-1955

BY LARRY STROBEL

To Kay
Best Wishes
Happy new year 2010
Larry Strobel

Copyright

Published by
Museum of North Idaho
P.O. Box 812
Coeur d'Alene, Idaho 83816-0812
www.museumni.org
(208) 664-3448

ISBN: 978-0-9825220-1-1

Cover: Coeur d'Alene from Tubbs Hill, 1949. Museum of North Idaho photo courtesy of Gene Hyde.

Book design, production and computerized image enhancement by
Moore Graphics Studio
smoore101@verizon.net

Book editing done by
Amy Shank

Table of Contents

About The Author

Larry Strobel is a fourth-generation Idahoan, born and raised in Coeur d'Alene, descended from two pioneer families who moved west to North Idaho in the late 1800s. Larry's prodigious memory served him well during forty years of work as a city mail carrier and helped him recollect his grandfather's stories of early days in Coeur d'Alene. Larry's humor, keen observations and love of music have enriched his life and make his stories memorable and enjoyable. Having spent twelve years as a member of the 560th Air Force Band (Washington Air National Guard) he continues to teach privately and play French Horn in several Coeur d'Alene bands and orchestras. His abiding interest in local history led him to the Museum of North Idaho, where he has served on the Board of Trustees since 1998. Larry and his wife, Sharon, have two grown children, Ronald and Shannon, and four grandchildren—musicians all.

Dedication

"When the Mill Whistle Blew" is dedicated to the memory of our longtime family friend, Louise Shadduck. Her unrelenting persistence in urging me to record our family history is the only reason this manuscript was started, researched and written. We will be forever grateful for her enthusiasm and encouragement as I struggled with a project much more complex than I realized at the beginning. Without her frequent pep talks and good-natured scoldings I would not have had the resolve to finish. God bless you, Louise.

Acknowledgements

The writing of a book, I soon discovered, requires much help from numerous sources. First and foremost I must thank my wife, Sharon, for her patience, ideas and her many hours of typing.

MaryLynn Gammel Strickland, my cousin from Renton, came for my mother's funeral in February 2001 and asked many questions about our family history. What I could tell her was enough to get her started, and her computer skills in genealogy improved dramatically as she extended her research back to the Mayflower. I give her full credit for her tireless efforts so productive in locating obituaries, death certificates, marriage licenses, census records and homestead information so essential to this writing.

My memory of English Composition classes taken at North Idaho College was nil, so tutoring from lifelong friend and retired English teacher Yvonne Deitz was of utmost importance.

Thank you to our friends, Shel and Al Stoner of Helena, Montana, for all their help researching the Montana Strobels. We spent three days with them scouring old newspapers, city directories and courthouse records, along with locating homesteads and gravesites. This led to the discovery of unknown cousins in Illinois with whom we have become close friends.

Museum of North Idaho director Dorothy Dahlgren deserves many thanks for her help with my research of local sites, dates, photos and events. I appreciate her encouragement and her expertise with publishing and marketing.

Thanks to the many friends and relatives who have refreshed and joggled my memory with bits and pieces of information. Some of those who helped were Louise Shadduck, Barbara Boughton Dennis, Del Gittel, Don Killian, Roger and Barbara Hudson, Kay Butler, Jim Abbott, Bill and Jean Hjort, Graydon Johnson, Paul Hakala, John Terris, Ace Walden, Ray and Helen Chatfield, Ralph Strobel, Valerie Strobel, Robert Butler, Ann Stowe Jordon, Robert Singletary, Art Randall, Don Johnston, Archie and Lorraine McGregor, George Hogeweide, Phyllis Hogeweide Swift, Dennis Strobel, Jack Strobel, Kay Powers and Bob Templin. Gwen Dreyer helped with determining the name of the book. Forgive me for anyone I might have inadvertently left out.

Thank you all for believing in me.

1 The Stowe Family

Somewhere in the deep recesses of each human mind is a point of first remembrance. My first memory is being in the kitchen of my maternal grandparents, George and Flora Stowe. From this point I can build many more memories of that log house located at 212 N. 18th Street in Coeur d'Alene, Idaho. But first, my intention is to explore the past as far as possible on both sides of my family. Then, with all the powers of my memory and the memories of other family members, plus the records that are available, I will try to construct an accurate account of how and why our family happened to end up here in Coeur d'Alene. So before I go forward I must go backward.

Research has taken us as far back as 1427 into the Stowe family history. The original Stowe family immigrants, John and Elizabeth, with their six children, arrived at Roxbury, Massachusetts on May 17, 1634. They came on the ship *Elizabeth* owned by one of John Winthrop's companies. The Dyer family who crossed paths with the Stowes many years later arrived only a few months behind them in 1635.

Descendants of John and Elizabeth were instrumental in the settling and development of New England. Their son, Thomas, helped found Middletown, Connecticut in 1654. Years later, Jonah and his cousins, Shelomith and Solomon, fought in the Revolutionary War. Author Harriet Beecher was descended from the original Stowe family, married her fifth cousin, Calvin Ellis Stowe, to regain the Stowe name that she used when she wrote *Uncle Tom's Cabin*.

Alanson Stowe, son of Solomon and Hannah Webster Stowe, was my great-great-grandfather. He was born December 25, 1799 at Croydon, New Hampshire and grew up at Morristown, Vermont. He married Achsah Burnam about 1823, and they became the parents of eight children, all born in Morristown.

My great-grandfather Solomon Asaph Stowe, the sixth child of Alanson and Achsah, was born June 26, 1836. He grew up in Morristown and, in the late 1850s, the Stowe family and their friends, the Dyers, moved to Salem, Wisconsin. On March 31, 1859, Solomon wed Mary Dyer there.

Born May 3, 1841, Mary Dyer was a bride at age seventeen. She was a direct descendant of Mary Barrett Dyer, a Quaker, who was hanged on the Great Tree beside the Frog Pond in Boston, Massachusetts. This earlier Mary had come to America to find religious freedom, but ironically, when she became a vocal advocate for Quakerism, she was arrested. She and her family were forced to move to Rhode Island where it was acceptable to be a Quaker. From time to time she would hear of her friends in Boston experiencing religious problems and she would sail over to help them. The fourth time she visited Boston and was once again arrested, her husband and son could no longer exert enough influence to free her from jail. In 1660 she displayed so much defiance she was sentenced to be hanged and was hanged May 22, 1660.

Mary Dyer; hanged on Boston Commons in 1660 for practicing Quakerism, pardoned in 1959. Photo courtesy of the State Library of Massachusetts.

Almost 300 years later when the old records were researched, it became obvious that this particular sentence had been unjust and a statue of her was erected on the grounds of the state house in Boston. On July 9, 1959 she was given a pardon.

Solomon and Mary's first son, Haven, was born in Salem, Wisconsin July 2, 1861. Three years passed, and they read a brochure advertising homestead land near Mapleton, Minnesota. The Stowes and Dyers all moved there in an attempt to escape the harsh Wisconsin winters. Mapleton located in the southern part of Minnesota was more suitable for farming. It was here that Charles Alanson was born July 29, 1866. Tragedy struck on July 21, 1867 when Haven was bitten by a rattlesnake. The bite was fatal to the six-year-old.

A third son, George Marshall, was born May 19, 1870. Lizzie Mariette came along April 30, 1874 and Edwin Dyer arrived October 10, 1877, all at Mapleton.

Solomon was primarily a farmer. Because of his religious convictions, he spent some time and effort studying to become a Baptist minister and before 1870 he was ordained. He and Mary desired to move farther west, but being conservative people, they resisted the temptation to join a wagon train. They thought it was unwise to risk the lives of their children in the months of hardship they knew would be involved.

The Northern Pacific transcontinental railroad was completed in 1883 and this changed everything. The railroad people printed exciting circulars about new territory, free land for settlers and gold strikes in the west. In 1887 the news of gold and homestead land in Idaho Territory was compelling enough to convince the Stowe family that the time was right to move.

Solomon heard of a place called Coeur d'Alene that had a much milder climate than Minnesota and was likely suitable for growing fruit trees. Fruit trees had always intrigued him, and at age fifty-one, he knew he had better get started if he was ever going to give it a try.

Solomon and Mary, still following their conservative inclinations, decided that he would take their two eldest sons, Charles and George, and ride the train to Idaho in the spring of 1888. If they liked Idaho the men would acquire land and build a house; then the rest of the family would come west. If Idaho was not to their liking they could retreat to Minnesota.

The promise of spring was in the air when Solomon and his sons, Charles, 21, and George, 17, stepped off the train at Rathdrum, Idaho Territory. The first week of March, 1888 would be a time they would always remember. They hired a driver with a wagon to transport them the 15 miles or so to Coeur d'Alene. They had all their personal belongings and the farm tools they had been allowed to bring on the train. The fee for the wagon was $1.50 per person for the trip, a rather steep price in those days. Before they got very far the wagon became mired in the mud, and the Stowes were pushing and pulling instead of riding. This soon prompted George to ask his father, "Why are WE paying HIM?"

The village of Coeur d'Alene wasn't very impressive, but Fort Sherman was. It was a self-contained unit, included a sawmill, and the fact that soldiers were nearby was a comfort. Coeur d'Alene Lake was even more beautiful than described and the forests appeared to be endless.

The next day brought good news. The man at the land office informed them that homestead land was not only available, but some of it was within a mile of where they were standing. Most people who had come to Coeur d'Alene kept right on going to the lure of gold or silver diggings at Murray, Eagle, Wallace or Wardner. The merchants who set up shop in Coeur d'Alene made their money from the soldiers at the fort and the stampeders needing a grubstake for the diggings to the east. Many boarded steamboats that provided quick and easy transportation to hoped-for riches. Agriculture and logging activities were barely underway.

The three Stowes took the available information and started walking. Solomon knew that to be successful he would have to find acreage with a ready source of that most precious of commodities—water. After considerable exploration they found just what they had envisioned located on one hundred sixty acres of mostly flat, heavily forested land with a good-sized creek touching the eastern boundary. The most exciting news was that pure, clear water bubbled out of large springs near the northeast corner of the property. This would be the location for their new home. They promptly named their place "Springwater" and this general area has gone by that name to this day.

News that a minister had arrived in the village spread quickly. When Emma Parsons Jordan died on March 13, 1888 the Parsons family asked Solomon to preach the funeral sermon and Charles Stowe and Blanche Parsons became acquainted. The Parsons were new to the area having come west from Blairstown, Iowa. Charles was 24 years old and Blanche was 20 when they eventually married on June 5, 1890 at Post Falls, Idaho.

Solomon excitedly wrote Mary a letter telling her to liquidate their property along with all belongings she couldn't bring on the train, and to plan on arriving at their new home about September 1. He hoped this would give the three men time to clear land, build a house and barn and get some vegetable seeds growing.

The gate to the Stowe place would ultimately be placed at the southwest corner of the homestead, which is now 15th Street and Pennsylvania Avenue. The western boundary extended north to the present corner of 15th Street and Harrison Avenue. The eastern boundary was approximately where Hill Drive is now located. The southern boundary was Pennsylvania Avenue. The northern boundary extended east from 15th Street and Harrison Avenue onto Stanley Hill, approximately the present intersection of Harrison Avenue and Royal Anne Drive.

Now the work began. The Stowes needed a team of horses and a wagon, rifles, a crosscut saw, axes, adze, peavey, chain, rope, block and tackle, shovels, a tent to live in and a stove, plus food supplies. A road good enough to get the wagon through to the house site had to be built. Solomon had the knowledge to accomplish this taming of the wilderness and taught his sons well. These were men who did not waste time. Saloons and card games were not on their agenda. Scripture reading and prayer started at daybreak and work concluded at dark. This routine had been taught to Solomon by his father and accepted by Charles and George as a way of life. Sunday, however, was another matter. That was a day to worship, read, write, and visit other settlers in the area and rest.

A log house took shape, built from selected trees on their property. They developed the springs into a workable water system and planted a garden to supply vegetables for winter. Plenty of meat was available for anyone who liked venison; deer-hunting season was twelve months long.

Finally the day arrived for the family to be reunited. On September 1, 1888, Mary, her mother, Anna Dyer, fourteen-year old Lizzie and ten-year-old Edwin stepped off the train at Rathdrum.

The trip to Coeur d'Alene was easy this time—the mud had all dried up.

At last the Stowe family was together in their new home. Mary had brought everything possible from Minnesota including seeds and cuttings from plants and bushes and a white rosebush that is still part of our family garden. The work had only begun, but they would proceed as a family. The only unhappy part of this reunion was the failing health of Anna Dyer, who died on September 17, 1888. Her grave is in the far southwest end of Forest Cemetery in Coeur d'Alene.

One day Solomon came home from the Mercantile and said he had discovered the town had no water mains. The residents had to get their water by collecting runoff from roofs or dipping from the lake. Neither method provided ideal drinking water. The Stowes' generous springs yielded a plentiful supply of pure, clean water, so George and Charles decided to go into business. They sold fifty-gallon barrels of water for 25 cents until a city water system was developed. The wagon was altered so they could haul the barrels without lifting them into the wagon bed. These two hardworking brothers also cut and sold cordwood for $2.50 per cord—hard work, indeed.

Part of the Stowe homestead included present-day Stanley Hill. The western edge of the hill was steep and was suited only for growing volcanic rock boulders and

Stowe family photo taken soon after their arrival in Idaho in 1888. Front row from left: Mary, Edwin and Solomon. Back row: Lizzie, Charles and George.

pine trees. A little farther east the soil was good; this is where Solomon planted his orchard. Apples and cherries did well here, and adjoining homesteaders planted many acres of cherry trees. This area is still called Cherry Hill. The orchards have been replaced with houses and it is a beautiful neighborhood.

It was not an easy process for a homesteader to obtain a patent and final ownership on his chosen 160-acre plot.

The Stowes had acquired their land in March, 1888, but didn't file their patent application until November 25, 1893. The filing fee was $22 and required four witnesses, family excluded, to fill out forms swearing they were well-acquainted with the applicant. The witnesses had to describe buildings constructed, fences built and maintained, acreage cleared and cultivated and estimated value of the improved property. Officials demanded measurements of the buildings, type of fence, indication of minerals, and proof that the settler had lived on the land continuously and acted in entirely good faith.

The four witnesses who completed the required forms for Solomon Stowe were Edward Stanley (Stanley Hill is named for him), John Fernan (Fernan Lake is named for him), Fred Empey and Edward Welch; the last two neighbors didn't manage to get anything named for them.

On July 16, 1895, the final papers were signed and duly registered. Application #426 was approved and the Stowes owned their land. Final Certificate #161 was issued on November 25, 1895.

The homesteaders directly east of the Stowes were of French descent, and this area was named French Gulch. It was discovered, after a time, that the soil of the western end of this gulch was of correct composition to be used for bricks. Enterprising Charles made a deal with the French family and opened a brick factory in 1901. This was not a small venture; capacity was ten thousand bricks per day. I have often wondered if he ever achieved his goal—that is a lot of bricks.

Charles and Blanche had five children: Milton, born May 16, 1891, Harry, born May 10, 1895, Earl, born March 6, 1897, Beryl, born March 13, 1903, and Clark, born March 16, 1905. Charles used some of his own bricks to construct a house in 1902. The present-day address is 2319 Hastings Avenue. It has been remodeled a number of times over the years and is presently occupied by the Brice Bemis family. The one-hundred-year-old bricks are doing just fine. In fact, it is a lovely home, helped by the designing talents of Jeanne Bemis. Thanks to efforts by Jeanne's sister,

Mary Dyer Stowe about 1906.

Barbara Boughton Dennis, the short street just north of the Bemis residence has been named Stowe Court as a tribute to the Stowe family. Charles Stowe and family later moved to Spokane and then to California.

The early 1900s found Solomon and Mary still living on their original homestead. They had logged the large trees over the years. Trees were cut during fall and early winter and then they waited for snow. Ideally, wet heavy snow would fall followed by a freeze-up. Then it was time to start delivering logs to the sawmill at the foot of 11th Street. A team of horses dragged the logs rather easily over packed snow and ice. A string of three to six logs per trip was common and, with any luck, a long freeze-up would occur.

Solomon enjoyed preaching for any occasion and was always available for weddings and funerals. He was often guest speaker at various churches on Sunday morning, including the Little Red Chapel on the old Fort Grounds. Finally, some of his neighbors decided he should have his own church. They proceeded to construct the church on the Stowe homestead on ground that is now the southwest corner of 23rd Street and Boyd Avenue. This worked well and he happily preached there until his death on July 15, 1909.

Obituaries of the day were much different from newspaper journalism in the twenty-first century. Solomon's included a lengthy prologue about his complaints of feeling faint and ill just before noon because he had singlehandedly moved his wagon underneath a cherry tree so that he could stand in it and pick fruit without a ladder and that he went into his house and lay down. The story continues about his feeling worse during the afternoon, and then he died. Apparently no medical help was sought.

Mary continued to live on the homestead after Solomon's death, but had a more modern home constructed near 23rd Street and Pennsylvania Avenue. This was a pretty spot with the creek rippling nearby. She lived there, with the help of her children, until her death on September 10, 1925.

The Farmers' Union converted Solomon's church into a hall, and was used as such until the 1950s. It sat vacant for many years and was finally torn down. A duplex occupies the property now.

Lizzie Stowe married Charles Williams in Coeur d'Alene on May 2, 1893. Their children were Florence, born March 12, 1894, and Lyle, born February 10, 1903.

Charlie was first and foremost interested in mining, and for the first few years of their marriage they lived at Wardner, Idaho and he worked for the Bunker Hill Mining Co. During these years his father, William C. Williams, also was employed there. Charlie became somewhat of an expert on rocks and minerals and slowly built a nice collection. His passion in life was prospecting and by 1905 he thought he had found the family fortune.

February 17, 1905 was a day of great significance to the Stowe and Williams families as Articles of Incorporation were filed for the Mineral Ridge Mining and Milling Company. The seven trustees were John Marshall, Emanuel Hoelzle, H. B. Stephens, Earl Sanders, Charles Williams, William Williams and Solomon A. Stowe. This hardworking farmer and devout Baptist minister who walked to church on Sunday carrying his Bible "just so" was no different from anybody else when it came to honest speculation and a chance to get rich in a hurry. It does seem out of character for him to

Solomon Stowe about 1906. Farmer, orchardist and part-time minister.

be involved in a mining venture, but it needs to be viewed from the perspective that he had been caught up in the excitement generated by the glib tongue of his son-in-law, Charlie Williams, a man who could have probably sold bags of ice cubes in an Eskimo Village. The amount of capital stock issued was $605,000 with each trustee receiving 100,000 shares, except Earl Sanders, who received 5,000.

The plans for this mining venture were complete and explicit. Water rights were secured, buildings were to be built, and a steamboat was to be acquired to haul supplies from Coeur d'Alene to the property and to move the ore from "the diggins" to the railroad.

Mineral Ridge is the mountain situated between Beauty Creek Canyon and Wolf Lodge Bay on Coeur d'Alene Lake. This was where Charlie spent a good deal of his time for the next twelve years, coming home when winter weather forced him out or when the family finances forced him to seek employment. For a time he was purser on the "Georgie Oaks" steamboat that made regular trips from Coeur d'Alene to the south end of the lake.

Charlie was anything but a con man. He wasn't lazy and he worked hard digging holes by the dozen on Mineral Ridge. He was on the right track – almost. The Caribou Mine was developed in Beauty Creek Canyon not far from his claims and was producing nicely until they came to a fault. The earth had broken and shifted, and the rich vein was never located again. This didn't stop Charlie and he kept digging holes, dreaming his dreams and telling his stories.

"No need to plant garden or cut firewood," he would tell Lizzie in the spring. "By fall we will be living in a big house on the South Hill of Spokane. We will have servants and buy the best of everything."

Lizzie and the children patiently planted the garden and tended their orchard. Brother George would drive into his sister's yard with his wagon loaded with firewood and quietly fill the woodshed. When winter came, Charlie would shake his head in disbelief that he hadn't hit his bonanza. Undaunted, he would get a temporary job and start planning for next spring.

The real testimonial to the sincere belief in this mining venture comes to light from the pages of Solomon Stowe's will. He left 27,500 shares of his Mineral Ridge stock to "The Christian Socialist" publication printed in Chicago, Illinois. This paper was an advocate of rights, work rules and fair play for the laborer and common working man. It preached many of the ideas that eventually were put into place by the formation of the trade unions. Solomon no doubt had a strong belief that the mine would prosper. He divided the rest among his three sons and wife. To his daughter, Lizzie, he bequeathed $5.00, apparently assuming that she would be wealthy from husband Charlie's share of the stock.

The Mineral Ridge Mining and Milling Company was dissolved in 1917. These claims at the very western edge of the Prichard formation either contain only small stringers of rich ore or the ore is so well-hidden it eluded efforts of all who worked so long and hard to unearth a bonanza.

Charlie and Lizzie Williams' house in Springwater was eventually sold and moved to 1720 Elm Avenue. It has been remodeled and is still there. The Williams had a modern home built at 614 North 15th St. where Charlie could happily sit on his front porch, visit, and watch the baseball games at Person's Field across the street.

Edwin Stowe married Adeline Hoskins Chapman at Coeur d'Alene in 1902. She had a son, Glenn, from an earlier marriage and Edwin adopted him. They had no children of their own. They lived on Edwin's share of the homestead where he farmed and also worked at the Rutledge Sawmill until his death on September 12, 1923.

Having completed this sketch of various relatives, I will back up and start the story of George M. Stowe, a man 20 years old, beginning his life as an adult in 1890 – the man destined to be my maternal grandfather.

George M. Stowe, always the enterprising young man, bought several acres of land in 1890 near the mouth of Silver Beach Canyon just east of Coeur d'Alene. Here, not far from the lake, he constructed an ice storage building. The walls and roof were insulated with one foot of sawdust. He had noticed that Fernan Lake froze over early every winter and at least some of the bays of Coeur d'Alene Lake froze over most winters. He would leave Silver Beach before dawn in his rowboat, row across the lake to Squaw Bay, and saw as large a block of ice from the frozen bay as his strength would allow. He accomplished this with a special saw invented for this specific purpose. He tied the ice floe to his boat and rowed back. This trip home typically cost him about three feet of ice from the front of the block due to wave action. His goal was to beach the ice at Silver Beach before nightfall.

The next day he would saw the ice into manageable blocks, then use his horse to drag the blocks to the icehouse where he would pack them in sawdust. This kept the ice from melting, even on the hottest summer days.

When the hot days of summer did arrive, he was ready for business. During the 1890s iceboxes were used in the kitchens of the finer homes, as these people were willing to pay well for ice delivery. There was no extra charge for seaweed, bark or dead fish that happened to get frozen into the ice. He never told me how much he charged for the ice.

One hot day, as he made his rounds with horse and wagon, he noticed a new girl working as a kitchen helper in the summer home of the Webb family, well-to-do Spokane people. The next ice delivery day he made a point of asking the cook about the new girl. He learned that her name was Flora Kinney and she was 18 years old. She didn't look that old. She was only four feet eight inches tall but, boy, was she cute.

So George went a courtin'. Flora knew he was serious when, after the summer home was closed for the season, he would ride his bicycle to Spokane to visit her. It was one of those bicycles with a large front wheel, very small rear wheel, and was propelled by pedals attached to the large front wheel. One revolution of that large wheel covered a lot of ground. Even so, as the road wasn't very good, it took most of the day to pedal to Spokane. Then he would check into a hotel and stay a night or two. This type of bike was not particularly easy to ride, and he took numerous spills on his journeys. Mud was a real problem for the narrow wheels and some days George was a bedraggled, muddy mess by the time he arrived at his destination. Later he changed to a regular bicycle, more manageable on the muddy roads.

Census records of 1890 list Flora, her sister Minnie, and their mother, Catherine, as domestics in Spokane. The whereabouts of Mr. Kinney were and are unknown.

George Stowe with his "modern" bicycle, much easier to control on muddy roads. Photo courtesy of MaryLynn Gammel Strickland.

George and Flora (Kinney) Stowe. Wedding picture, January 1896.

Obviously, Stowes and Kinneys had one thing in common—they were hard workers. Maybe this was part of the attraction. They were a handsome couple and on January 8, 1896 they were wed in a ceremony held at a Protestant Episcopal Church, the All Saints Cathedral in Spokane, Washington, with Reverend Dean Babbitt officiating. The witnesses were Etta Davis and Minnie Kinney. George was 25 years old and Flora was 20.

George and Flora's first home was situated in Silver Beach Canyon, a short way up the creek from the icehouse. The present-day address is 1452 Silver Beach Road.

This marriage would eventually produce seven children. Their first son, Bryan George, was born May 6, 1897. Both George and Flora wanted a big family and George always had a knack for quieting fussy babies with his gentle ways. Ruth Muriel was born September 27, 1898, with Floyd Asaph following on October 27, 1900.

Many farmers of the time had large families and perhaps the theory was that children grew into farmhands available for many years. Gordon James arrived September 21, 1902, followed by Ena Mary on June 6, 1905. Beulah Genevieve, destined to become my mother, was born May 6, 1910. Five years later, May 31, 1915, Doris Katherine arrived, completing the family.

George, like his father, Solomon, was interested in fruit trees and had acquired land suitable for orchards about 1895. He didn't travel far to get it. The land, just east and north of Silver Beach, was steep and rocky near the lake, but leveled out on a sizeable bench about two thousand feet up the hill from the lake. This was railroad land, and he bought eighty acres. The price was one dollar per acre. There was a good spring on the western edge of the bench land that could be developed into a cistern. This land was perfect for orchards; it faced south and was above the valley floor, assuring direct, daylong sunshine. This meant warmer days and nights, which translate into a longer growing season.

George started clearing land and had plans for a new house, but was frustrated by his inability to find a way to build a road to their new property. Every approach was stymied by a large basalt (volcanic rock) outcropping. He laid out various routes, but if he raised the elevation enough to go over the rock, the road was too steep. Their growing family outgrew the Silver Beach bungalow, so he took time to construct a log house on his share of his parents' homestead. It was square and was always called "The Square House." It was located in the vicinity of present-day 18th Street and St. Maries Avenue. This house was larger, but was inconvenient because it was too far from his new orchard.

It became urgent he build a road somehow. Finally, he blasted the southernmost edge off this troublesome rock point, and picked away at it until he had a narrow roadway. Now they could build, but they did not get moved in until 1906.

Their house was a two-story log structure with spacious front and back porches. It was unique in that the logs for the walls were set on end then the logs were covered with four-inch overlapping siding so the final product didn't look like a log house. The view was spectacular. They looked straight south up the lake and southwest into Kidd Island Bay. Tubbs Hill blocked their view of downtown Coeur d'Alene.

They dug a large root cellar into the hillside near the house. This was similar to a cave and was fitted with a heavy, tight-fitting door. The idea was to keep the temperature cool and constant in all kinds of weather. Meat, vegetables, fruits, butter and milk had to be kept from freezing in the winter and spoiling in the summer.

The Stowes' good friend and neighbor on the next hill to the west, George Armstrong, argued good-naturedly about who had the best view. Probably the best of all was the view from the Sid Streator home on Rutledge Hill, but his land wasn't suitable for orchards.

George had started clearing his land as soon as it was purchased—an ongoing project for at least thirty years. Trees suitable for saw logs were cut, dragged to the lake by a team of horses, floated to the sawmill at the foot of 11th Street, and sold. George was disappointed that so many of these heavy, pitchy yellow pine logs sank to the lake bottom before they reached the mill. These "deadheads" were a waste of time with no profit. This was not a get-rich scheme, anyway, as the logs only fetched about $9.00 per thousand board feet delivered to the mill.

The land to be cleared resisted George at every turn. He tried burning the stumps, but that only succeeded in turning them black most of the time. He discovered that well-placed stump powder, when he could afford it, would split the stump and then a fire was more apt to be effective, and with any luck would burn for a month or more, spreading far out into the roots. Uncle Gordon's comment years later was that pulling stumps with a horse was a good theory, but in reality was only a good way to blow off steam and use a lot of cuss words, and he never knew of anyone who actually removed a stump that way.

George cleared land up the hill north of the house to be used as their vegetable garden and discovered a sand and gravel bar resembling a beach. On this "beach" he found several Indian arrowheads. Apparently this had been the shoreline of a huge body of water that covered this whole area in ancient times.

A grub hoe was his main tool used to dig out bushes, roots and sod. A grub hoe is a heavy hand tool with a three-foot handle. It is similar to a pick, the difference being that instead of a head with two sharp metal points, it has a horizontal four-inch blade on one side of the head to cut sod and small roots, and a vertical blade on the other side of the head to use as an axe. The effectiveness of this tool is determined by the strength and accuracy of the person swinging it. George was an expert. His favorite technique was to back into a bush or small tree and push it over as far as possible while grubbing through the outer roots to get the grub hoe underneath. As soon as the taproot was severed, the tree or bush came out with little resistance. To clear an area twenty feet square and rid it of roots was a good day's work. He was not a big man—about five feet seven inches tall and one hundred and forty pounds—but he was long on know-how and determination. He worked from dawn 'til dusk six days a week.

Part of his property was prepared to plant oats and hay, which required further work. Plowing new ground was torture, as the horse-drawn plow bounced off roots and rocks and threw the farmer around like a rag doll. Then a harrow, a flat, heavy implement with iron spikes sticking straight down, was pulled through the plowed ground by that same weary horse. Small roots built up under the harrow until the spikes were raised out of the dirt. Then George had to stop, clean out the roots and pile them up to be burned.

As soon as he had a small area cleared and cultivated he would plant more apple trees. He planted a few at a time as the clearing progressed. He worked so hard that, by his own admission, some nights he was so tired he didn't know if he could climb the porch steps to get into the house.

A few years later he had twelve acres of apple trees plus four acres of sweet cherry, plum and peach trees. The Wegener (Wagner) and Jonathan apple trees made up the bulk of the orchard, but he also grew Rome Beauty, Gano (Red Delicious), Wealthy, Early Harvest, Grimes, Golden, Rhode Island Greening, Winter Banana, Yellow Transparent, and an early apple called Strawberry. George grew Bartlett and Flemish Beauty pears along with cherries. He wasn't satisfied with just a few cherries, but planted Bing, Lambert, three kinds of Royal Ann, May Duke, Late Duke, Montmorency pie cherries and Tartarian, which was valuable as a pollinator. With all these, plus plum and peach trees, George was a true orchardist.

George eventually hired the Newell brothers and other loggers to clear the part of his land unsuitable for farming, so money could be raised to buy more land. By about 1905 he decided to purchase the eighty acres adjoining his property to the east. When he returned from town he was visibly upset as he stomped into the house. "Consarn it Flora," he yelled, "They doubled the price on us. I had to pay two dollars an acre."

George worked off the farm only when the need for dollars became urgent. He was known to take work on road construction or house construction, but could usually get by with what he raised or shot.

One job he did take was to help move the Fort Sherman Hospital that had been bought by Immaculate Heart of Mary Academy. It was to be placed at their new

State of Idaho Orchard Inspector in Stowe orchard about 1910.

school site at 9th Street and Indiana Avenue. The fort was dismantled in 1905, and this large three-story building was jacked up and placed on large timbers called "skids." Then logs six to eight inches across, selected carefully, with little or no taper from end to end, were placed under the skids and out in front of the building. A team of eight horses then pulled the building as it rolled on the logs. After a short distance the logs that rolled out behind were picked up and carried back to the front. Then they rolled ahead a few more feet and repeated the procedure. Progress was slow, but it worked. George was one of the log movers and worked for two weeks until the old hospital was in place at its new location. This building was used as classrooms and living quarters by the nuns at IHM Academy until the early 1960s when it was razed to make room for new, modern buildings.

George planted mostly dwarf apple trees that produced heavily while still young. These small trees were easy to spray and pick. The orchard flourished and by 1910 was producing handsomely.

A picture dated November 23, 1911 shows George at the National Apple Show in Spokane, Washington. He had approximately five hundred boxes of apples on display and won first prize.

The following year he shipped a railroad boxcar of apples to Oshkosh, Wisconsin where his cousin, Cecil, acting as broker, was to sell them for a better price than could

George Stowe apple display at National Apple Show in Spokane, WA, Nov 23, 1911. Mr. Stowe is second from left and is pictured with inspector and fruit-grower officials.

Bryan, Floyd and Gordon Stowe in the family orchard about 1910.

be had in Idaho. It was a good theory, but railroad shipping costs were excessive and he did not do that again.

The local market could absorb about 2500 boxes of apples each year, as the Dalton Gardens, Hayden Lake and Spokane Valley Orchards were not yet developed. For many years, a lot of his apples were sold in St. Maries, shipped by steamboat. A wooden apple box measured 12 inches by 19 inches by 11 inches deep. A full box weighed forty pounds and sold for about 40 cents.

These were prosperous years for the Stowe family. In a period of fifteen years George had turned forestland into this thriving orchard. The land was not irrigated, which made his orchards vulnerable to years of drought, but most years precipitation was adequate. The children were old enough now to contribute many hours of labor.

George built a large, well-designed apple sorting and storage barn below the house adjacent to the road. Part of the north rock wall of this building is still intact as I write, if you know where to look.

Though they were living only about one mile from the eastern edge of Coeur d'Alene, there was no electricity available nor was it available for the twenty-nine years they lived there. They did have a telephone, a line built and maintained by the farmers of the area. It was known as the Sunnyside party line and was connected to the main line of the telephone company, referred to as "Central," officially known as Postal Telegraph and Cable. The Stowe phone number was 6F2-4, and their ring was two long and four short. The phone was vital to the Stowes because so many of their fruit orders were called in, but calling required patience with about a dozen homes on the line competing for phone time. Everybody's phone rang for every call to the line, and whoever heard the phone ring had to listen carefully to see if the combination of long and short rings was theirs. Privacy was nonexistent, as neighbors listened in whenever they felt like it, and might even add a comment or two. If the line was busy and one needed to make an emergency call, the parties talking could always be asked to hang up. Perhaps this is one reason why this type of line was referred to as a co-operative (co-op).

It was about this time, when the boys were teenagers, that they were working with their father building a new fence north of the house to create a pasture for the animals. They had borrowed some new-fangled equipment from a neighbor, namely a posthole digger and a wire stretcher, which were a big help. It was hot and dry, but suddenly Bryan discovered he was pulling up moist dirt. A little farther and it was downright muddy. George started yelling with excitement. This was their lucky day—they had stumbled onto a spring. Their water supply had been tolerable, but this spring had real potential.

The next Sunday George's brother, Edwin, came to the ranch to help because he was considered an expert "water witcher." Witching was done with a forked stick cut from a good-sized bush; actually it looked like a big slingshot without the sling. One side of the fork is held in each hand, with the main stem of the stick pointing straight out ahead. The theory is, when you walk over water hidden in the ground the stem will dip down. The more water, the harder that stick will jerk downward. (Don't laugh; it really works.) Edwin crisscrossed the area and after a time said, "Dig here."

They dug a hole about eight feet deep right into a stream of water just waiting to be set free. George dug a reservoir, bricked it up and covered it with a concrete lid. He ran a pipe to the house and they had running water, a luxury few farmers of the day knew. This water supply never failed them, and their water-carrying days were over.

George, an inventor at heart, was always looking for ways to make life easier. He decided there must be an easy way to shuttle food around to nine people at mealtime without having to continually ask, "Please pass the __." He nailed some one-inch boards together and cut them into a circle (wheel). This wheel, about twenty-four inches across, was set on a base about eighteen inches in diameter, grooved to hold marbles so it turned easily. Just set the bowls of food on the wheel and turn was his theory. But this didn't work very well because the marbles would bunch up and squirt out of the groove, allowing the wheel to tip, which meant someone might receive an unexpected bowl of food on his or her plate. So he tried casters, and they worked much better. Now, if you needed spuds, you quietly turned the wheel until they arrived and there was no need to interrupt a conversation to ask for food. This was the forerunner of the "lazy Susan" of later times; an efficient way to serve a large family and the kids loved it.

Times were good in 1911 and the family had some extra money. They bought a Clayton upright piano, which our son and his family are still enjoying in their home today. George bought a red (the color) White (the make) truck that rolled along on wooden-spoke wheels with narrow, hard rubber tires. This White truck lasted until

Stowe children, 1913. From left: Gordon, Ruth, Beulah, Floyd, Ena and Bryan.

1924 when he converted it into a hay wagon and he then bought the largest Ford truck made at that time. George needed a big truck because he had bought more acreage several miles east in the Sunnyside area and developed more orchards. This land is now called Vista Heights.

In the year 1915 the Stowes decided to purchase two lots at 1424 Lakeside Avenue and build a winter home there. This would eliminate a three-mile walk to school for the children. They had saved some money, and George contracted to have a two-story house built on the corner lot. This made the walk to school less than a mile which was a real relief in bad weather. The total cost for land and house was six hundred dollars. This house is still in good shape and was re-roofed again in 1999. The second lot at 1422 Lakeside Avenue has a much newer house on it. This meant they made two moves a year and they always had the challenge of moving the piano in and back on the big truck.

The fruit trees had to be sprayed, of course, and the boys were required to help. A hand-pump in the wagon supplied the pressure for the sprayer, and the boys didn't exactly fight over the right to pump next. One summer day George noticed that aphids had moved in and created a huge problem. The boys groaned at lunchtime when George informed them tomorrow would be a spray day. That afternoon heavy winds developed, and a dust storm blew in making visibility so poor the lake could barely be seen from the house. The next morning when they checked the trees the aphids were gone; the dust had smothered them. It is indeed an ill wind that blows no good.

The Stowes did have off days, as all families do. One summer day when Floyd was twelve he got into a heated argument with his mother and announced he was leaving home. She said he was free to go; so he wrapped up a few clothes, hooked them to a stick and took off. This happened about eleven in the morning. Late afternoon rolled around, and he showed up at the back door and told his mother he had decided to return home. It seemed he had seen enough of the world and I suppose he was hungry. He did his best to save face as he pointed at a cat sleeping on the kitchen floor and said, "Boy, that cat sure grew a lot while I was gone."

It was early spring of 1916; Charlie Williams' excitement and enthusiasm had reached the boiling point. He was convinced, after a winter's worth of thought, he knew right where to dig and "the big strike" was imminent. Unbelievably, George, a normally conservative man of well-thought-out logic, got caught up in Charlie's rhetoric. He announced one evening he had decided "to go and help Charlie for a little while." His reasoning was that there wasn't much orchard work that time of year and the boys could manage.

Flora, usually quiet and soft-spoken, didn't hesitate. "Is that so?" she snapped. "You have seven children and you aren't going anywhere!"

End of idea.

Stowe and Barnum Families get-together at Stowe ranch house about 1920.

February of 1926 brought unseasonably warm weather. So warm, in fact, that the sap came up in the apple trees. It appeared that an early spring was on the way which would mean a big crop coming up. Then the fickle north Idaho weather had a field day. In March the temperature dropped to sub-zero and the beautiful orchards were destroyed. The "Apple King of North Idaho," as some people called George, was shot out of the saddle. His major source of income was gone and his empire was wiped out in two days.

There was nothing to be done except cut down the trees and start over. George was now 56 years old and it was too late in his life to start a new apple orchard. Several areas in central Washington State had been developed for apple growing including the Okanogan valley area, Wenatchee, and Cashmere, where the climate was much better for apple orchards. A few years out of the market would have left George unable to compete as the Washington farmers flooded the market and drove the price down. He was beat and he knew it.

He was down but not out. After careful calculations he decided to replant and specialize in Mont Morency pie cherries. These trees were hardier than apple trees, grew quickly, and he knew he had a close and easy way to sell all the cherries he could raise. Seiters Cannery, eight miles away at Post Falls, would take them all. He planted several acres and this orchard was highly successful until the early 1950s.

George did replant a variety of apple trees just east of their home to provide apples for family and friends. This also gave him an opportunity to experiment with grafting, as he attempted to develop a perfect apple. Some of these trees on the hill are still bearing fruit; they are gnarled and untended, but haven't given up.

The loss of the orchards was a financial blow, but the worst part was the heartbreak he endured while cutting down the trees he had nurtured so carefully. By 1926 only two of the seven children were still at home, Beulah and Doris, so he did most of the clearing and replanting by himself.

Girls didn't have much opportunity to earn money in those days. When George bought a new cook stove he told Beulah that she could have the old one. He told her to clean and shine it up and he would haul it to town, sell it, and she could have the money. So her project began. She polished and cleaned and worked for several weeks until the old stove sparkled. The day came to take the stove to town and they loaded it into the truck. This was an exciting day for Beulah, but trouble was lying in wait. George was uncharacteristically in a hurry that day and neglected to tie the stove down. When they made the sharp right turn from their driveway onto the road, gravity took over, and the stove toppled over and fell out of the truck. The hill was quite steep below the road, and the stove rolled over and over until it hit a tree far below. The only thing left was the nameplate and a pile of iron. That was about as bad as it could get for a teenage girl in 1927. She still talked about that day when she was eighty years old.

Beulah graduated from Coeur d'Alene High School in 1928, the only one of the seven children to finish high school. She had attended grade school at the Lakeview School located at 1422 Young Avenue. This building is now an apartment house and is in surprisingly good condition.

In those days many teenagers didn't see any reason to finish high school. All the

Beulah Stowe high school graduation picture.

Doris and Beulah Stowe about 1930.

Stowe children had the opportunity, but the boys could get mill jobs or woods jobs from about age fourteen on. The girls often married young and school just didn't seem to be important, so long as they could read, and write and figure. Some had to go to work to support the family.

During the early 1900s deer season was whenever the need for venison arose. As this area became more populated a deer season was imposed, and someone called a "game warden" was signed up to enforce it. This didn't do much to stop farmers from shooting deer; it just made them a lot more careful about when and where they did the shooting.

One summer Sunday afternoon the Stowe ranch was the setting for a family dinner. Along in the afternoon somebody spotted a deer in the orchard. It was quickly decided that some fresh venison was in order so a bullet was dispatched in the direction of the unsuspecting deer. The wounded deer took off down the steep hillside with the men in hot pursuit. The deer arrived at the top of the long embankment above the highway where the hunters almost had him when he gasped his last, toppled over, and rolled into the ditch below. While they debated what to do, a truck stopped, two men jumped out and loaded up the deer. They pulled a tarp over it and took off. George and family peered through the bushes watching their deer being driven away and could do nothing but wave goodbye.

Sometime in the late 1920s George had some bad luck with his eyes while cutting a piece of barbwire in the woodshed. He laid the wire across a double-bitted axe stuck in the chopping block and smacked it with a hammer. A piece of the wire flew into his left eye and resulted in blindness. Several years later, a stick of wood bounced and hit his right eye, causing partial blindness. This didn't stop him from his usual daily hard work, but his poor eyesight did make life more difficult. He continued to drive his truck in spite of Flora's protests, but there wasn't much traffic and he got along all right until 1944 when he was forced to quit driving.

In 1935 George turned sixty-five and decided it was time to retire from the ranch. He sold the property to daughter Ruth and her husband, Jasper Hogeweide. He and Flora bought two large lots at 212 North 18th Street in Coeur d'Alene. The large house at 1424 Lakeside had been sold after the loss of the apple orchard.

George cut selected red fir trees at the ranch, tall with little taper, and hauled them to their new home site. The skills he had learned as an eighteen-year-old came in handy once again as he squared the logs with a broad axe and dovetailed the corners. It was a small house but it had an attic-like upstairs with bunks for sleeping built into the wall and a door that opened to a balcony over the good-sized front porch. The back porch was quite large and covered. A door lifted up on this porch floor to access steps to the cellar. The inside of the house was mostly kitchen where everyone congregated to enjoy the warmth from the cookstove and to visit or play checkers. The living room was tiny, mostly taken up by a bed for guests. The one bedroom was small, as were the bathroom and pantry. The garage, woodshed and workshop combination, built east of the house, was considerably larger than the house.

In early 1936 George and Flora moved in. The house was completely surrounded by flowerbeds and there was no lawn; he thought grass was a waste of time and water. The yard was all gardens with potatoes, sweet corn, green beans, ground cherries,

Stowe house and garage about 1937.

peas, popcorn, cucumbers, carrots, parsnips, cabbage, lettuce, spinach, beets, onions, turnips and lots of squash. Anything that would grow in North Idaho could be found somewhere in his garden. Several crocks of pickles were always brining in his cellar and the entire attic of the garage was a drying area for popcorn. He invented a crank machine to shell popcorn, and he never had to chop kindling wood because he used the popcorn cobs to start fires. East of his garage he set up an area where he experimented on grafting apple trees; his continuing goal was to create a perfect new apple.

Then George bought an acre of land at 310 North 20th Street and made a garden out of the whole thing; mostly he grew potatoes and squash there. This land had no water supply available and he cultivated regularly to bring the moisture up. Dry land farming is a challenge, but he was successful most years.

Did I mention that George was now retired? In his spare time he would work at the ranch helping Ruth and Jasper and their five children who now lived there. They had built a new house in a long draw at the east end of the property. There was no view of the lake but a good water supply determined the house location; a good water supply doesn't always come with a view.

When it was time for the cherry harvest, George spent long, contented days in the orchard he had created working with his grandchildren, Jasper Jr., George, Phyllis, Donna and Walter Hogeweide. This was still a fine orchard and a tribute to his hard work. Later in the summer and fall he sold his vegetables to the grocer at 12th Street and Sherman Avenue. This was the only source of income for George and Flora in these days without social security checks. If you think about it, real retirement was impossible.

Flora and George Stowe in 1937 at their new home, 212 North 18th Street.

2 The Strobel Family

Research on the Strobel family prior to John George Strobel's immigration application in 1851 has not yielded any useful information. Strobel is a common name in Germany with at least four different spellings. Literally translated, it means "a large shock of hair."

Great-grandfather John was born in July, 1813 in Bavaria, Germany and his wife-to-be, Verena Walser, was born February, 1837 in Wuertenberg, Germany. She immigrated to New York in 1855 at age eighteen and spent the next two years living in New York and Cincinnati, Ohio. Why she and John moved to Elkader, Iowa is unknown, but apparently that was where they met. They were married on December 19, 1858, an unlikely union – he was forty-five and she was twenty-one. He was established in business as a shoemaker; perhaps, (let's use our imaginations) they met when she needed her shoes repaired.

The census records of 1860 show John and Verena's first child, Louis, was born in January of that year. Their second son, John George, was born July 17, 1861. This is the ancestor I will focus on because he became my grandfather. To avoid confusion he was referred to as George and he used this name even on official documents for the rest of his life.

Verena had a total of nine pregnancies with six of the children surviving infancy. Along with Louis and John George there was Gustave born in 1866, Robert in 1868, Mary in 1870 and Laura in 1876. Mary was the only one who did not achieve adulthood, dying at age twelve in 1882.

The 1870 census lists John not only in the boot and shoe business; he was into a partnership with another man as a saloonkeeper. The year 1880 finds John still listed as a shoemaker with no mention of the saloon. Perhaps that had been an ill-advised venture. The entire family was still in Elkader except nineteen-year-old George, whereabouts unknown to us.

The western move was soon on for the family. Gustave moved to Butte, Montana in 1885 when he was nineteen years old and was employed there by the Journal Publishing Company as a printer from 1886 to 1892.

Louis had followed his father into the boot and shoe business in Elkader. However, he is listed in the 1888 city directory of Puyallup, Washington as an employee in a restaurant owned by Olivia Kelly, a widow; the directory of 1889 states that Louis and Olivia are co-owners of that same restaurant.

By the year 1890 Olivia Kelly has married Theodore Worthington, owner of a general store and she is listed as a fruit grower. Louis is listed as a gardener in her employ. Records are sketchy, but the sequence of events takes on the look of a modern-day soap opera. Next thing we find, Mr. Worthington marries a Mrs. Crasker, and on November 6, 1893 Louis and Olivia are wed. He is now thirty-three and she is forty-two. Olivia bore a daughter, Florence, in January of 1892. The identity of her father is unclear, but she was raised as Florence Strobel.

John George, Verena, Robert and Laura moved west to the Clancy, Montana area in 1892 and by 1893 they are living on a ranch several miles up Clancy Creek. Gustave joined them there, and lasted two years as a rancher and part-time miner until 1894 when he moved to Helena, Montana, where he was employed by the State Publishing Company of Helena. He eventually became president of the publishing company and married Charlotte Ashman of Philadelphia on June 27, 1899. John George died in 1903 and is buried at the Jefferson City cemetery. Verena, Laura and Robert were all ultimately buried in the family plot there.

Meanwhile at Willow Wood, Ohio, Phillip Gruber and Emma G. Pinkerman were married on April 1, 1871. Their first child, daughter Emma Celestia Gruber, was born January 8, 1872 at Willow Wood. When she was fourteen in 1886 she moved with her parents and brother, Ira, to the Hamilton, Montana area. This is where she met George Strobel who has finally shown up after being invisible for thirteen years. He is a miner there and their marriage certificate is dated July 2, 1893 at Curlew, Montana, a rough and tumble mining camp; he was thirty-two and she was twenty-one.

Celestia's mother's name was Emma, and to avoid confusion she always went by the name Celestia, the same as John George went by George. How curious it is that two people who went by their middle names would marry.

Due to the fact that family stories and available records don't agree, it becomes a rather difficult chore for this writer to give an accurate account of the lives of George and his family between 1894 and 1900. We do know their daughter, Alma Estella, was born in Victor, Montana on March 23, 1894.

Fortunately the family appears in the 1900 census and they are living at Wardner, Idaho where George is employed at the Bunker Hill Mine. They had endured sadness; a baby girl, Beulah, was born May 3, 1895 and died in infancy as so many babies did in those years. By 1900 Alma was six years old and Ruth, born September 26, 1899, is seven months old. Tragedy struck again and Ruth died before she was a year old.

The Union Pacific Railroad was completed through the Coeur d'Alene River Valley in 1889 and whatever year the Strobels moved to Wardner was their introduction to this beautiful fertile valley. We can imagine their enjoyment and awe as the train passed through Harrison, a thriving picturesque town supported by the payroll of six sawmills and numerous logging companies. From the mouth of the Coeur d'Alene River the tracks turned east and never ventured far from the banks of the deep, slow-moving river. The settlements of Springston, Medimont, Lane, Rose Lake, Dudley, Cataldo, Kingston and Enaville were all prospering thanks to lumbering and farming. Enaville was located at the confluence of the North and South forks of the Coeur d'Alene River and marked the eastern edge of the valley.

Though George had been a miner in Montana and was headed to a job at the Bunker Hill mine, he and Celestia surely were impressed by the lush dark green grasses giving way to tall and stately fir and pine trees extending into the mountains as far as they could see. Small lakes scattered throughout the valley included Thompson, Anderson, Blue, Black, Swan, Cave, Medicine, Killarney, Bull Run and Rose. Each of these sparkling gems was unique in shape and color, all teeming with fish. It was perfect for waterfowl and birds of many species enjoying unlimited feeding and nesting spots.

Sometime shortly after the visit by the census taker at Wardner, George, Celestia and surviving daughter Alma moved down the valley to Lane, Idaho. Perhaps the labor unrest, metal price fluctuations, and frequent turmoil in the Kellogg, Wallace, Wardner area were not to their liking as steady employment was not the norm. Perhaps the death of two daughters dictated a change of scenery. Perhaps the availability of sawmill, logging and agricultural employment which were safer and healthier than mining influenced their decision to move. All are logical.

The town of Lane was situated almost exactly halfway up the Coeur d'Alene River Valley on the south side of the Coeur d'Alene River. A large sawmill was located adjacent to the river, with the town extending up the hill overlooking hundreds of acres of farmland with a glimpse of Killarney Lake nestled between two large mountains.

Town of Lane, Idaho in 1907. Museum of North Idaho photo.

Now a new direction for the Strobels was underway. Homestead land was still available, and in 1900 they applied for a parcel of land on the north side of the Coeur d'Alene River about two miles downstream from Lane. An S-shaped bridge crossed the river at Lane and connected with the road on the northern bank. This road bridged the outlet from Killarney Lake near its juncture with the river. This "creek" was referred to as the Killarney Ditch. The original creek had been dredged to accommodate the movement of saw logs from Killarney Lake into the river. The Strobel land fronted the river and was 155.7 acres rather than the customary 160, probably due to a curve in the river.

The rich black soil was extremely fertile and my dad, Earl, talked about hay that grew so tall men disappeared when they walked through the fields. He told about cabbage fields growing huge cabbages and lush strawberry farms employing many pickers. The farmers would row to Lane in rowboats at daybreak to pick up workers for the day. The farmers harvested vegetables in season and shipped via railroad three times each day to markets in Spokane and beyond.

The Strobel house was located several hundred feet from the riverbank and their place soon became known as Strobel Meadows. The process of "proving up" usually took about seven years and they were right on schedule when the land patent was awarded on April 10, 1907.

John Wilbur was born August 13, 1901 at Lane and Earl (no middle name), who would become my father, was born August 12, 1905, also at Lane. He speculated they couldn't decide on a middle name so he went without.

There are no records to indicate where George was employed until 1907, but he probably worked at the sawmill. That year he and a Mr. Grimm started construction of a logging railroad into the mountains from the southwest corner of Killarney Lake. This project started with a pier and eventually extended into the wilderness for six miles.

I marvel at the fact that a locomotive and flat cars equipped to haul logs were barged to this remote roadless area and unloaded from the barge onto the new tracks. This had to have been a monumental project considering the equipment available. Tracks had to be laid through extremely rugged and heavily forested terrain with hundreds of

Celestia Strobel with dog, Jerry, at Strobel Meadows homestead near Lane, Idaho about 1904.

Earl Strobel, about 7 years old in 1912.

stumps needing removal. I suspect dynamite was one of their best friends.

They logged as they cleared land and laid track. The logs on the flat cars were unloaded on the pier, splashed into the lake and arranged in long narrow booms to be pulled by a tugboat through Killarney Ditch into the river. A boom of logs can be any number of floating logs enclosed by "boom sticks," which are peeled logs with a hole drilled through each end to accommodate a heavy chain and metal bar to hook the boom sticks together. A boom could be any size or shape depending on the width of the waterway to be traversed. Logs have to be carefully controlled or they end up like runaway children—all over the place.

Pilings for the pier are still intact and solidly in place as I write – February 2008. The decking has rotted and is long gone. I wish there were records of money spent and by whom, size of crew, time involved, equipment used, acreage logged, amount of timber harvested and profits made. There are no records to indicate how long the railroad was in operation. I truly wish I could have known this grandfather. He had a mechanical engineer's mind, was an extremely hard worker, and had a knack for getting the job done in spite of seemingly insurmountable obstacles. This will become even more apparent as we progress with this history.

My father could recall the evening the Lane sawmill caught fire when he was almost four years old, sometime in 1908. They were still living on the riverbank and he recalled they had just started their evening meal when the mill whistle began to blow continuously. George jumped up so fast he overturned his chair and yelled "The mill is on fire!" A brick had been hung on the whistle cord and it continued to blow until consumed by the fire. Every able-bodied person in the area rushed to fight the fire, but it was no use and the mill was destroyed. It was not rebuilt, and this started the long, slow, steady decline for the town of Lane.

Perhaps this fire eliminated the market for George's logs, although they could still have been floated to the mills downstream at Harrison. It would seem, however, that the end of the mill was the end of the Strobel-Grimm logging operation and

Lane Lumber Co. Mill at Lane, Idaho about 1905. Museum of North Idaho photo.

the Strobel family moved to the head of Killarney Lake. They built their house in a short narrow gulch off the northeast corner of the lake near an excellent year-round spring. We know their home was established before July 11, 1910 because this was the birth date of Gladys Elizabeth, their last child. Access was by boat only, and when it became apparent that the baby was about to arrive, nine-year-old John was sent in their rowboat to pick up the midwife at Lane. This was at least a two-mile row each way and he was instructed to hurry. The midwife commented later that she had never seen a boy that age row with such urgency as the boat lunged forward with every dip of the oars.

Their move to Killarney Lake was dictated by at least two reasons. The Post Falls Dam was completed in 1906 and this raised the summertime level of Coeur d'Alene Lake to 2128 feet above sea level. Previous uncontrolled summer levels fluctuated somewhere between 2100 and 2110. The dam had a major effect on the Coeur d'Alene River Valley because the water flow to drain the area was considerably diminished. The threat of flooding was greatly increased and, for all practical purposes, they now lived on a flood plain. Each high water was depositing mine waste and raw sewage from the Kellogg area on the once-fertile land, and their house on the riverbank was no longer a safe or sensible place to live. A series of dikes and ditches were constructed to reduce the problem in part of the valley, but were not practical for the Strobel property.

Dikes were built around a field with ditches dug just inside the dike to collect water that ran off the field or seeped through the dike. This was effective for moderate high water which is the case most years. However, the dikes meant nothing in the years when a real flood came roaring through the valley. Parts of the railroad track would be submerged; chunks of the rail bed would wash out, leaving the tracks and ties hanging in midair with water covering the valley from mountain to mountain.

George and Celestia had acquired at least sixty acres at their new home site. George either made a lucky find and bought the land, or bought the land and made a lucky find. On the steep hillside, scarcely one thousand feet northeast of their house, he discovered a "blow out" of mineralized rock similar to, but not as extensive as, the discovery by Noah Kellogg (Bunker Hill Mine) and True and Dennis Blake (Sunshine Mine), both near Kellogg, Idaho. Now the experience George had acquired as a miner in Montana and at Bunker Hill would be put to good use.

George was now forty-nine years old, Celestia was thirty-eight, and it was time to seize this opportunity to make their fortune. Obviously, excitement ran high and visions of great wealth danced in their heads as they planned carefully.

The logistics for mine development at this site appear to have been of mindboggling difficulty. Access by water meant that all machinery and supplies had to be barged. This would have meant railroad transportation to some point, perhaps Coeur d'Alene or possibly Lane, where ore cars and track, motors, building materials, timbers, etc. had to be off-loaded onto a barge. The hardest problem, however, was to unload the barge at the Strobel property and then move this extremely heavy equipment up a steep grade for about 1500 feet. A narrow road was constructed on the north side of the gulch to accomplish this, but I can only imagine the effort and ingenuity involved.

By the time May of 1915 rolled around, they had made so much progress that the Strobel Mining Company was required to file an annual report with the Idaho Geological Survey. They weren't the only people in the area chasing mineral wealth; they were listed as being in the Medimont Mining District. George Strobel was listed as president and general manager of the company, with R.L. Black as secretary. Mr. Black, presumably, was a financial backer.

They had incorporated and issued 1,000,000 shares of capital stock, par value $1.00 per share. They had 300,000 shares of treasury stock on hand, and had sold $1,400 worth of stock at 10 cents per share. Obviously friends and neighbors believed this was a viable venture as they spent their hard-earned money to buy stock. It is unlikely that it was marketed beyond the immediate area. We have been unable to locate a Strobel Mining Company stock certificate.

A mine tunnel of five hundred feet including crosscutting had been dug. Their equipment included one twenty-horse-power gasoline engine, one Ingersoll Rand compressor, one Ingersoll Rand drill, machine house, blacksmith outfit, rails and ore cars. The tunnel was timbered to prevent cave-ins. There was an average of four employees during that year, with the miners being paid $3.50 to $4.00 per day and the mechanic paid $5.00 per day.

The bad news was that they had no reduction plant; consequently they had shipped no ore, had no gross revenue and, of course, paid no dividend.

However, the silver and lead prospects were interesting enough to get the attention of the Bunker Hill Company at Kellogg. After all, this was still the Pritchard formation, the same mineralized rock that was so rich in the Wallace, Kellogg, Mullan and Pinehurst areas. Could this be just as rich? Somebody thought so.

Later in 1915 the Bunker Hill Mining Co. offered the Strobels $72,000 for their property. The deal would be $12,000 down payment, with a $12,000 payment every six months until it was paid off. If, at any time, Bunker Hill decided the mine was not going to be profitable, the Strobels would keep whatever money had been paid and could have the property back. It appeared all their hard work had paid off—that was a lot of money in those days.

George was eager to sign the papers and at fifty-four years of age move on to an easier life. But there was a problem. Celestia refused to sign, insisting, "If our mine is that good, we should work it ourselves and make some REAL money."

The 1916 annual report to the Idaho Geological Survey shows the Strobels making progress. They had now sold 40,000 shares of stock at 10 cents per share for a total of $4,000 in two years. They were still working all three claims, but show their acreage as forty. Had they sold twenty acres? I think so, because later maps show another mine called the Gray Eagle just east and adjacent to their claims.

The report shows another two hundred fifty feet of tunnel work, which must have included a separate one-hundred-foot nearly vertical shaft, dug to the west and downhill from the main tunnel. There is still no mention of any ore being sold. There are still four employees at $3.50 per day. Interestingly, this report is not notarized. Even though the report is typed, there is a handwritten note at the end. It read: "Note—It is here very difficult to reach a Notary, hence I send it on so as to avoid delay. Hope it is satisfactory. Geo. Strobel." This is the only sample I have of my grandfather's handwriting.

There was no report filed in 1917. George became ill and was soon bedridden. He failed rapidly and died July 30, 1917 at the Killarney Lake home. He was only fifty-six; burial was at Lane Cemetery.

Now Celestia was in big trouble. Alma had moved to Spokane, Washington to work and go to college, but three children were still at home living in a house that could only be accessed by rowboat and had no electricity or telephone. Their spring on the hill nearby had been dug out and the walls rocked up, but I don't think water was piped into the house. Money was scarce and John soon began working in the woods sawing logs. Celestia's decision to not sign the agreement to sell their mine must have haunted her for the rest of her life.

There is a 1918 geological survey report filed for the mine. It had been incorporated under a new name—the Coeur d'Alene-Spokane Mining Company. I find it almost implausible that Celestia had convinced her brothers-in-law, Gustave and Robert, that she had a rich mine, but somehow she did it. Gustave is now president and Robert is secretary of the new company. By this time Gustave was president of the Montana Publishing Co. of Helena, Montana; he and his wife, Charlotte, were prominent citizens there. Robert and Laura, neither ever married, along with their mother, Verena, owned a large cattle ranch near Clancy, Montana.

Celestia was a tall, stately woman about five feet, nine inches in height; she wasn't afraid of hard work and was stubborn and determined. However, it appears she really didn't understand the difficulty of drilling and removing rock from a mine tunnel. It occurred to me that at this point it would have been extremely interesting if she and Uncle Charlie Williams could have met. After all, he was digging holes with only a fraction of the prospects she had in a mountain fifteen miles away, but with the same strong beliefs. George had been a stocky five feet six inches tall. He was the driving force, the one who got the job done. I don't think she realized just how much he had accomplished, how smart he was or how hard he worked.

There is no doubt in my mind that Gustave and Robert and the entire family believed whole-heartedly that this mine was the "real deal" and that a fortune was within reach.

By spring of 1918 the paperwork was complete and Gustave and Robert were prepared to get the mine work underway. But on June 26th their mother, Verena, died at Clancy, Montana and they had to focus their attention on business at home. Gustave continued the payment of taxes on Celestia's property so she wouldn't lose it.

Reports were filed with the Idaho Geological Survey for 1918 and 1919 which indicate their desire to continue mining. But there were many problems; Gustave had a job and a family in Helena, including wife Charlotte and twins Edgar and Irene, born September 6, 1902. Edgar was epileptic and Gustave's own health had begun to deteriorate.

A newspaper article dated July 12, 1918 tells the story of sixteen-year-old Edgar Strobel falling out of the second-story window of Dr. Wirth's dental office onto the sidewalk near the Antler's Theater. He was reaching for a flag and lost his balance, startling the people on the sidewalk who rushed to the boy's side, thinking to find him dead or dying. Fortunately he came out of the fall with nothing more than a broken

Robert Strobel, Clancy, Montana cattle rancher, miner and Jefferson CO. treasurer. Photo courtesy of Robert Butler

Laura Strobel on right, unknown lady on left, Montana homesteader. Photo courtesy of Robert Butler.

wrist and shock. They took him to Dr. Lanstrum's office for treatment and he avoided his dental appointment for that day.

Anything except a short absence from home would have been a hardship for Robert also. His land holdings were considerable with his mother's homestead added. Verena had received the patent for her land only four and a half months before her death. Now only Laura was available to take care of the property when Robert or Gustave left.

Gustave Strobel on left with son-in-law Edward Butler in 1920. Photo courtesy of Robert Butler.

Irene Strobel Butler, daughter of Gustave and Charlotte, in 1920. Photo courtesy of Robert Butler.

When a Montana cattle ranch is mentioned, visions of flat wide-open range land come to mind. Not the case with the Strobel ranch, which was located about three miles up Clancy Creek from the town of Clancy. This property was mostly steep hills with an abundance of boulders and pine trees. Only twenty-two acres of bottom land was suitable for hay and this was seeded to Timothy hay. A large barn, a milking shed and two houses, one on each side of the road, plus several cabins gave the place the look of industrious people hard at work. They obviously had an interest in mining there also because they dredged the creek looking for gold.

All this wasn't enough for Robert; he developed political ambitions, eventually leading to his election as Jefferson County Treasurer. He died at Alhambra, Montana in 1963 at the age of ninety-four. Laura died in Helena in 1959. She was eighty-two.

Gustave died Aug 6, 1922 and one would be inclined to believe that would have ended the "Montana Strobels" interest in the Killarney mine, but that wasn't the case. Gustave's probate papers show entries in Charlotte's ledgers of "payment of taxes on the Killarney property" and "travel expenses for Robert's travel to Idaho for Killarney Lake Mine business" every year until the probate was completed in 1934.

Did they believe? The answer is a resounding YES!

Even though reports were filed for several years in the 1920s, no actual mining ever occurred. Later reports used the term "prospect" in place of "mine." By 1938 the mine was renamed "The Crystal Mining Company." A new owner had a post office box in Cataldo, Idaho as his address; the dreams and paper shuffling continued and no work was done by him either.

Barn at Strobel Homestead near Clancy, Montana (picture taken about 1960).

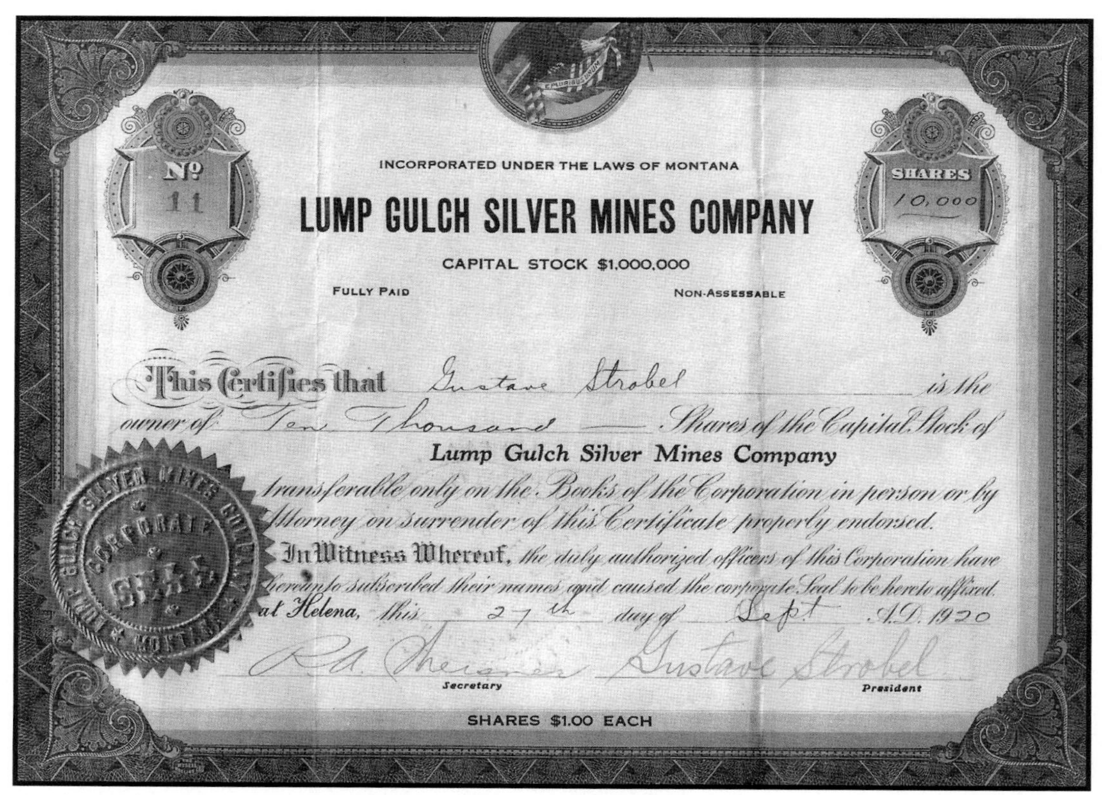

INCORPORATED UNDER THE LAWS OF MONTANA

No 11

SHARES 10,000

LUMP GULCH SILVER MINES COMPANY

CAPITAL STOCK $1,000,000

FULLY PAID NON-ASSESSABLE

This Certifies that Gustave Strobel is the owner of Ten Thousand — Shares of the Capital Stock of

Lump Gulch Silver Mines Company

transferable only on the Books of the Corporation in person or by Attorney on surrender of this Certificate properly endorsed.

In Witness Whereof, the duly authorized officers of this Corporation have hereunto subscribed their names and caused the corporate Seal to be hereto affixed at Helena, this 27th day of Sept A.D. 1920

[illegible] Secretary Gustave Strobel President

SHARES $1.00 EACH

Stock certificate from Lump Gulch Silver Mines. The Strobel brothers were serious in their efforts to develop this property. Certificate courtesy of Robert Butler

In 1940 the Geological Survey people inspected every old mine they could get into. George's tunnels were still accessible for 650 feet including crosscuts, just the way it was the last day he worked. The vertical shaft was filled in, no doubt for safety purposes. This rather extensive report notes that ore content ran heavy to lead and not very good for silver. Wide veins were of short length and rapidly pinched down to only a few inches. It was good enough to create excitement and hope that the next few feet of tunnel would hit "the good stuff" as it had at Sunshine and Bunker Hill. It was good enough to quicken the pulse of anyone with an interest in mining, but was it really there? We will never know. The land eventually reverted to the Bureau of Land Management.

Meanwhile, back to 1919. I suspect life for Celestia was financially difficult, to put it mildly. Fourteen-year-old Earl took a job sawing logs with a crosscut saw as John had done two years before. This brought some money into the family coffers. By this time her mother, Emma, had come to live with them and this probably was an additional financial responsibility. Emma's husband, Phillip Gruber, had disappeared somewhere along the way; he died prior to 1880. She later married Solomon Shirey, a carpenter from the Hamilton, Montana area; obviously this marriage did not work out because by 1909 he was living in Coeur d'Alene, married to Hannah Nettleton.

The 1920 census shows Celestia, three children, and her mother living at Killarney

Emma Gertrude Pinkerman Gruber Shirey about 1885. Photo courtesy of Helen Strobel Chatfield.

Lake. Later that year disaster struck. One evening a family member, carrying a candle for light, went into a bedroom closet and must have unknowingly touched the candle to a garment. Nobody ever knew for sure how it happened. Suddenly Earl noticed a light flickering through the gap under the door. He jumped up, jerked the door open, and was greeted by a wall of flame. The family ran for their lives; none of them was injured, and they watched helplessly as their home was reduced to ashes. Gone were all records and ledgers. Gone were the photographs, the keepsakes, what little money they had, all household furnishings and all their clothes except what they were wearing.

Somehow the house on the riverbank had survived the 1917 flood that raised havoc all through the valley. The Lane Bridge had been washed out and now access was by boat only. I know the five of them moved back into this house because Ray Chatfield, Cousin Helen Strobel Chatfield's husband, has memories of visiting this Strobel home in the mid-1920s when he was a young boy.

John married Mildred Felardeau December 26, 1923, and moved to the Rose Lake area several miles up the valley. Earl lived in various logging camps most of the time and sawed logs. His sawing partner for many years was Arthur "Jack" Lethby, a man who had immigrated from England. They were an unlikely pair; Jack was noisy and brash and liked to visit the taverns and whoop it up when he emerged from the woods; Earl was quiet and shy and took his paycheck home to his mother.

The nearby town of Lane had faded into the sunset; the burned sawmill had not been rebuilt and repeated flooding which washed mine tailings downstream from the Kellogg, Wallace, Mullan, and Burke areas had poisoned the rich farmland. The twenty-five-piece town band, the lively coming and going of train passengers, the loading of fruit, vegetables and hay onto the train several times a day and the boisterous taverns were all fond memories. The beautiful river had been ruined and fish could no longer live in the polluted water. Some families considered Lane their home and found ways to make a living. Names such as Moe, Crawford, Lapp, Goodson, Tanner, Donahoe and Soucy were prominent for many years; some are still there.

Emma Pinkerman Gruber Shirey died July 19, 1926 at age eighty-two and was buried in Lane Cemetery. The cemetery lot cost $5.00 and was not paid for until more than a year later. Money was scarce.

The story was that Emma did not trust banks and, after the Killarney Lake fire, did not like the idea of having money hidden in the house either. This was the reason, rumor had it, that she sewed very deep pockets into all her dresses and always carried her money and valuables with her. My cousin, Helen Strobel Chatfield, has one of her dresses and, sure enough, the pockets are long and deep. Maybe she didn't have such a bad idea, after all.

Alma had left the Killarney Lake home before George died and sought work and education in Spokane. She worked for a doctor and her goals were attained as she graduated from the State College of Washington at Pullman on June 11, 1928 when she was thirty years old. She was awarded a degree of Bachelor of Science in Bacteriology and a degree in Home Economics. On March 17, 1929 she was awarded a diploma from the Dickinson Secretarial School in Spokane. She was one intelligent, ambitious lady.

Alma Strobel, college graduation picture, 1932.

Gladys Strobel high school graduation picture, 1929. Photo courtesy of Charlotte Nelson Hawley.

In 1929 she was still employed by the medical doctor, Dr. Eugene Gay, who had evidently helped her financially with college expenses. When he moved to California she followed him with the promise of a better-paying job. By 1930 she was working in the laboratory in San Joaquin General Hospital. Dr. Gay became involved in the opening of a medical laboratory in Petaluma, a new innovation then, and after working at this lab for a few years Alma became manager. When the opportunity arose she became the owner. Medical tests performed somewhere other than doctors' offices were becoming customary. Strobel Clinical Laboratory developed into her life's work and she became very successful.

The 1930 census reveals Gladys living in Spokane, Washington working as a waitress. Her mother, Celestia, is living at the same address, 3002 W. Diamond, and is employed as a cook.

After much searching in the wrong places we found a marriage license issued on June 13, 1930 in Spokane, Washington to Walter R. Andersen and Gladys Strobel. His age is listed at thirty-three and her age is listed at twenty-two. After more research we discovered this document is filled with inaccuracies; her age is actually nineteen and his is forty-three, Andersen was misspelled Anderson, Gruber was misspelled Grover, it was not Walter's first marriage (though he states that it is), and his place of birth, St. Paul, Minnesota, does not agree with other documents. So much for that, but we're not done yet!

We discovered another marriage license for Walter issued in Spokane and he claims he was born in Wisconsin. It seems that by 1930 he has forgotten his marriage to Florence Westmark on November 13, 1916 and the subsequent birth of their two daughters. The 1920 census also reveals he was born in 1887. He was employed as a railroad brakeman on both certificates.

I can only guess Gladys probably thought she would be considered too young for Walter if she was still a teenager and that she made an error on her mother's maiden name. But I also conclude that Walter was trying to hide his past for reasons known only to him.

Gladys and Walter lived near US Highway 10 at the eastern end of Fourth of July Canyon and had no children. Family stories I remember say he was killed in a car accident sometime in the 1930s and she moved to California to live near Alma and her mother by 1935. She worked as a secretary and enjoyed the warmer climate. She didn't intend to remarry, but eventually she met a good man, Lester Nelson, in Redding, California and they married July 17, 1948. They had one daughter, Charlotte Ann, born October 15, 1949.

The 1930 census also lists John, Mildred and their four children living near Clagstone, Idaho. Wilbur had been born July 1, 1924 followed by Helen on May 3, 1926. Walter came along August 14, 1927 and John (Jack) was born May 5, 1929. Earl was living with them; actually, he was living in a tent in their yard. The Strobel brothers had been attracted to this area 35 miles north of Coeur d'Alene, thanks to the availability of log-sawing jobs that lasted virtually year round. They worked in a long valley northeast of the busy, prosperous town of Spirit Lake. Hoodoo Valley – also known as "The Hoodoo"—was a loggers' paradise thanks to huge yellow pine trees on fairly flat terrain with little underbrush.

Panhandle Lumber Co., Spirit Lake, Idaho ca. 1930. Museum of North Idaho photo.

The Panhandle Lumber Company in Spirit Lake, Idaho built one of the biggest and best- equipped sawmills ever seen in North Idaho in 1908; costs exceeded $500,000, a huge investment for those times. It appeared to be worth it as they seemed to have all the ingredients for a successful, long-term lumbering operation. The Idaho and Washington Railroad delivered logs and hauled the finished lumber to market. Besides the Hoodoo Valley, the company owned vast forest lands, much of it on the eastern slopes of Mt. Spokane. Their log supply seemed assured for many years and it was happy days for the Strobel brothers. At last, steady employment had come their way—a hard-to-come-by circumstance in the logging business.

However, sawmills have a common difficulty. On August 11th, 1931 a fire started in a lumber shed and spread rapidly. Several hundred thousand board feet of lumber were destroyed, an estimated loss of over a million dollars. This, of course, stopped all work while plans to rebuild were formulated.

John and family moved back to Rose Lake and Earl went back to logging camps on the North Fork of the Coeur d'Alene River.

A historical footnote seems in order here. This fine mill was rebuilt and operated successfully until August of 1939 when a massive forest fire, allegedly started by huckleberry pickers, roared through their timber holdings on Mt. Spokane and onto the mill grounds. The devastation was complete as most of the mill buildings, log decks and lumber piles were consumed. This was the knock-out punch nobody ever wants to see. The mill was not rebuilt and hundreds of workers lost their jobs. This signaled the rapid decline of Spirit Lake, Blanchard, Vay and Clagstone.

Celestia's time of residence on the riverbank ended about 1929 with her move to Spokane where she could find employment. At last she lived in a residence that had electricity and running water. It had to have been a relief to move from the riverbank where the threat of flood-waters was a scary, uncertain way of life. The

Celestia Gruber Strobel about 1934.

Earl Strobel and Beulah Stowe in 1934.

From left, John and Doris Gammel, Beulah and Earl Strobel at ranch in 1935.

inevitable happened in December, 1933; exceptionally heavy snow fell in the early part of the month followed by heavy rain and unseasonably warm temperatures. This combination triggered one of the worst floods ever recorded in the Coeur d'Alene River drainage destroying the old Strobel homestead house on the riverbank.

By 1933 Celestia was renting a house at 1025 Lakeside Avenue in Coeur d'Alene. She had a job at the Pines Bakery located at 409 Sherman Avenue. She had only six blocks to walk to work, which was a necessity since she didn't own a car and had never learned to drive. Mildred came from Rose Lake to stay with her mother-in-law in early March, 1934, as the birth of John and Mildred's fifth and last child approached. Betty was born in that house on March 11, 1934.

Earl continued to work and live in logging camps. He made many lifelong friends along the North Fork where he maintained a string of trap lines during the winter when logging was shut down. His closest friends were the Baslingtons and he often stayed with them when he went to check his trap lines. The sale of the pelts, mostly muskrat, provided some much-needed wintertime income.

Earl met Chet Boyer in one of the camps and they became good friends. Eventually he was invited to the Boyer home near Silver Beach east of Coeur d'Alene for Sunday dinner. Fern Boyer, as a woman is often inclined to do, decided to try her luck as a matchmaker. She talked Earl into taking an evening walk up the hill to the Stowe ranch. It just happened that Beulah Stowe was over twenty years old and didn't have a boyfriend. In the eyes of a matchmaker, this was an opportunity; so two of the shyest

Mother's Day, May 12, 1935. Front, Flora Stowe and Celestia Strobel. Back, Beulah Strobel and Earl Strobel.

people in North Idaho met that day. Fern knew this might be a match if either one of them could ever think of anything to say. They were both from pioneer families so that was a good starting point.

Earl worked up enough nerve to visit the Stowe ranch the next weekend when he was in town and to make a long story short, they were married on Earl's twenty-ninth birthday, August 12, 1934. The wedding was at the Church of the Truth, 523 E. Garden Avenue, in Coeur d'Alene with Reverend Erma Wells performing the ceremony.

Earl and Beulah bought a ramshackle little house on two fifty-foot lots at 1503 Coeur d'Alene Avenue for $600. The mortgage payments were exactly $8.00 per month and the mortgage was held by Lake City Investment Co., 102 N. 4th St., owned by Harold V. Wilson. This house needed help immediately, especially the roof with its aged crumbling cedar shingles. Guess who showed up with tools, nails, shingles, and lots of know-how? George Stowe came chugging down the street in his black 1924 Ford truck and their roofing project was soon underway. He also made sure there were vegetables in the cellar and wood in the shed for their first winter together.

Earl went to work at the Winton Lumber Company sawmill at Gibbs, Idaho. This

Winton Lumber Co. Sawmill at Gibbs, Idaho provided employment for Earl Strobel and several other family members. Museum of North Idaho photo.

mill was located on the north bank of the Spokane River, just west of where Coeur d'Alene's Mill, Davidson and LaCrosse Streets terminate. This meant he could be home every night and his logging camp days were over. The only problem was, the mills ran out of logs in the wintertime and closed down for several months. His employment was reduced to snow shoveling and odd jobs, and that $8.00 house payment looked mighty big.

Earl was resourceful (a polite word for scavenger at this point), and he started

Oslund Maternity Home, 102 Indiana Avenue.

collecting material for a garage and woodshed. He salvaged used lumber from houses being torn down, and rescued board trims at the mill before they made it into the burner. He accumulated enough to build a two-story structure set on timbers placed on large rocks. It was good enough that it withstood the elements for sixty-six years.

This was still the time of the Great Depression. Adolf Hitler was stirring up big trouble in Europe and the Japanese were showing strange and worrisome behavior in the Pacific. Earl had only two years of formal schooling and limited job skills. Beulah was educated through high school, but had never worked except at her parents' ranch. Earl had nearly died in childhood from an illness and was so thin that his friends at the sawmill referred to him as "old hatchet ass." Beulah was four feet eleven inches tall, weighed seventy-nine pounds, and had always tended to be frail. Should this couple attempt to bring children into the world? Would they have the abilities to raise children in this environment?

Their decision was YES. Surely the troubled world would calm down, the financial difficulties smooth out and the job markets improve. They had faith.

I was born March 31, 1937 at Oslund Maternity Home, 102 Indiana Avenue, Coeur d'Alene, Idaho. This must have been a busy place, as many of my schoolmates were born there also.

This was a difficult time for Beulah. The complications of birth left her bedridden for three weeks, and Earl called upon various relatives, friends and neighbors for help in caring for me. But the Strobel-Stowe combination had strong ancestry, and with their love and faith they were survivors.

3 Childhood

My first memory is being in the kitchen of my maternal grandparents' house at 212 N. 18th Street when I was three years old. The most important recollection of my early life, however, is that I felt safe and unthreatened. Along with my parents to look after me, I had three grandparents, eight uncles, nine aunts and more than thirty cousins. For the most part, all of them treated me in a kind and loving manner.

Larry Strobel, one year old.

Some early events are hazy in my mind, but a few are still quite clear.

The year was 1940 and Dad had just traded cars. It was an emotional time for Mom and she was crying because she didn't want to sell our older Ford. I was in the back seat of our "new" car, a 1929 black four-door Model A Ford, and Dad kept telling her everything was all right, and that she would soon become acquainted with the new car.

September 1940 was eventful. A bed was set up at the west end of our living room and the furniture was rearranged. I suspected something was about to happen and, sure enough, on the morning of the 23rd when I came out of the bedroom there was a big white basket sitting behind our wood-burning heating stove. I peeked in and saw a baby. He was my new baby brother, Ralph Milton, and I was quite impressed by his full head of black hair. I had slept through the night and hadn't heard a thing. A midwife came to our house, sparing the expense of a maternity home.

I was confused when I had to leave that morning to stay with Uncle John and Aunt Doris Gammel, but I soon figured out this was going to be fun. I went in their car with Uncle John to his job of the moment—not many men had a steady job in those days. He was digging a basement under a house located somewhere in the 600 block of Coeur d'Alene Avenue. He backed his trailer under the end of a narrow conveyer belt that went into a hole underneath the house. We went downstairs to the basement and when he turned on an electric motor the conveyer belt started to move. I watched as he hand-shoveled dirt onto the belt and it disappeared up and out. It was time to go when the weight of the dirt in the trailer made the car set low in back. We took the dirt to their house at 319 N. 20th Street, and he shoveled it into low places in their backyard. This was fun, and I had a little shovel so I could "help."

I was in no hurry to leave three days later when it was time to go home. My big redheaded uncle treated me very well and Aunt Doris was a terrific cook.

After I got home my baby brother, Ralph, cried a lot because he had something called colic. Mom got a little bit cranky when I asked if I could go back to Aunt Doris's house.

Sometime later we had a little excitement. Mom labored for hours to make a lemon meringue pie. This was tricky to accomplish with a wood-burning cook stove and a crying baby. Finally, the pie was done, it was a work of art, and she set it on the back porch to cool. We had a chicken coop with eight or so chickens at the time, and when Mom stepped out to bring in the pie our banty rooster was perched on the edge of the pie plate, pecking away at that most appetizing fare. Mom grabbed her broom and swatted him with all her ninety-nine-pound might. The pie landed upside down on the floor as the rooster tried to escape. If a chicken could smile that rooster would have been smiling as he squawked and fluttered away. I thought Dad was never going to get Mom calmed down. The next day she made another pie and cooled it in the house. As for the rooster, he was a "marked man" (fowl), and Mom had her revenge when he ended up as the main course for next Sunday's dinner.

I was about four years old when Dad decided we needed a new outhouse. The dilapidated model in use was across the garden on the northwest tip of our property. A lot of shoveling was needed when the snow came, and it was an easy target when the mischievous neighbor kids went on a toilet-tipping spree.

Dad attacked his newest project with great zeal, first cutting a hole in the woodshed wall and installing a door. He dug a hole about eight feet deep and lined it with creosote-treated two-by-six boards. Next he borrowed a cement mixer and poured a four-inch-thick concrete floor. The stand, seat, and lid (yes, it had a lid that closed) were constructed of varnished two-inch boards. The outhouse was in the corner of the woodshed so he had to build only two walls. The roof was handy to pile wood on from the woodshed side. There was a modern toilet paper-holder and, "ta da," an electric light for those early morning and nighttime visits. Just pull the string and the light came on. Our house wasn't much, but our outhouse could be classed as a Cadillac. If it had been heated, it would surely have been "all-world." It was safe from toilet-tippers on Halloween.

I wasn't one to stay put in our yard, and no amount of scolding or spanking could convince me to quit wandering off to visit the neighbors. I was told this had started before I could walk. I was between one and two years old when Mom discovered I was nowhere in sight. She raced around the neighborhood frantically looking for me and found me playing happily in the yard at 320 N. 15th Street, a crawl of at least two hundred feet. I was slow to learn how to walk, but a real whiz at crawling.

When I was four, Dad decided the best way to solve my wandering ways was to build a fence. He planted large wooden posts, and attached five-foot-high wire fencing to them. Two gates with latches I couldn't reach effectively trapped me in our front yard. That was what they thought anyhow. Dad was proud of his handiwork, and watched me through the window as I inspected this hindrance to freedom. I can still remember noticing a depression under the wire near the front gate. I lay on the grass,

Ralph and Larry Strobel, 1942. Strobel house and garage at 1503 Coeur d'Alene Avenue in background.

rolled over a couple of times, went right under the wire, and was on my way. I didn't get very far before Dad's heavy hand was on my shoulder. A load of dirt solved the problem, and they finally had me trapped.

A vivid memory occurred on December 7, 1941—Pearl Harbor Day. I had a little tricycle and, since the weather was stormy, I was in the house riding back and forth between the living room and the kitchen. Dad had the radio going full blast and kept telling me to be quiet. He tried to explain to me what was happening, but it was a bit much for a four-and-a-half year old to grasp. I did understand that I should be mad at somebody called "the Japs." I can remember President Franklin Roosevelt talking on the radio when he announced that the United States was now at war. World War II would dominate our lives on a daily basis for nearly four years. I was old enough to understand this was a frightening, sad and bewildering time. Important lessons to be learned were patriotism and love for the United States of America. I was soon being taught the Pledge of Allegiance, and Kate Smith was frequently heard on the radio singing "God Bless America."

In mid-1942, when I was five, the subject of rationing came up and before long the date of implementation was announced. Gasoline was one of the items to be rationed, so Dad and Mom decided it would be real nice to visit Uncle John and Aunt Doris; they had a new baby girl, MaryLynn, born July 7.

It was a cold November morning when we started off for their home in Renton, Washington. This would be our last chance to visit for a long time, perhaps years. We were all excited about the visit as we "sped off" in our 1929 Model A Ford. None of us realized how long this day would be. Freeways did not exist and cruising speed for our car was about 42 miles per hour. This made for a long day to complete a three-hundred-plus mile trip, even without complications.

We were out in the desert of central Washington when the right rear tire went flat. Dad put on the spare and we were on our way. About an hour later there was a loud "bang," and the spare tire was blown to bits. Mom was rapidly slipping into her panic mode, but Dad seemed calm as he removed the original flat tire from the wheel and patched the inner tube. He aired it up with his hand pump and we were ready to roll.

Mom was completely unnerved, started crying, and wanted to go home. Dad wouldn't hear of such a thing and we continued west. I have never decided whether he was brave with great faith or just foolish. We forged ahead even though Ralph and I got carsick. The back seat was soon an unpleasant place. We kept going. It got dark and we started the long pull over Snoqualmie Pass as it started to snow. Before long a highway patrolman stopped us because chains were required to travel over the pass. Dad put chains on the rear wheels and we kept going. By some miracle we got through without any more flat tires.

Finally, about 11 pm, we arrived at the edge of Renton. Dad got out the map Uncle John had drawn for us and promptly discovered that map-making was not one of John's talents; we soon became hopelessly lost. Dad spotted a house with a light on and decided to ask for directions. Now our luck picked up. A teenage boy gave him clear and concise directions to the Gammel residence and we were soon parked in their driveway.

We went into the house and everybody was excited and talking at once. Uncle

Doris and John Gammel in 1942. Photo courtesy of MaryLynn Gammel Strickland.

John and Aunt Doris had given up on us as lost forever. I crawled up into a big overstuffed chair, leaned back, and the next thing I remember I woke up in a bed and it was daylight. I think that is the only time in my life I don't remember getting into bed.

The next day Uncle John and Dad were lucky enough to find a store that still had tires for sale and they bought a new spare plus an extra. Tires were getting hard to come by as the war effort took over the country.

Several days later we headed for home. We encountered no snow and no flat tires. Ralph and I weren't carsick either. We left in the dark and arrived home in the dark, but it was by comparison an easy trip. I suppose this trip had a lot to do with my reluctance to travel as I grew older.

The war was the dominant subject of conversation day after day, and even youngsters like Ralph and I who had both parents at home were affected. Don and Doug Taie, two of my good friends with whom I played frequently, were really jolted. Their dad, Lyle, was drafted into the army and went away to fight in Europe. Their mother, Frances, was nervous, unhappy and frantic with worry. Unfortunately, one day his name was listed in the MIA (missing in action) section of the Coeur d'Alene Press. He never came home. I felt sick to my stomach for my friends and their nice, pretty mother and this made a lasting impression on me. I hated the war and what it was doing to people.

In 1943 Dad was thirty-eight years old. Men were being drafted into the army at a rapid rate, but he was considered too old, as were all of my uncles. Some of my older cousins were drafted; Jasper Hogeweide, Willy and Walter Strobel and Jack Stowe went. All came back alive.

Rationing became a big issue. Each registered family was mailed a coupon book every three months. The coupons were labeled A, B and C for different months, and were required for the purchase of certain merchandise, such as sugar, coffee, tobacco, nylon stockings, whiskey, oil, tires and gasoline. Gasoline coupons could be saved for months so a family could take a trip if they wished.

If a person could afford to buy only five pounds of sugar, but had a coupon for ten pounds, he or she was given change in the form of red, green or blue tokens, about the size of a dime. Each color had a different value. If one had enough colored tokens they would equal a coupon.

When a grocer made a deposit of money at the bank, he also made a deposit of coupons and tokens he had taken in. He got a receipt, which he used to prove to the government he had sold a certain quantity of an item, and this was the only way he could get more inventories. My friend and source of information, A.K. "Ace" Walden, was assistant manager at the Kellogg branch of Idaho First National Bank at the time, and he declares that this was the worst bookkeeping experience of his lengthy banking career. Counterfeiters sprang up, and then the banks were required to check the coupons with a special light, which added to the bankers' nightmare.

The shortage of sugar was a considerable concern for families like ours because Mom always canned many jars of cherries, pears, apricots and peaches. On one of Aunt Doris's visits she was helping Mom can some peaches and they ran out of sugar.

Aunt Doris still had her sugar coupon for that month, and volunteered to use it so that the rest of the peaches could be canned. She borrowed our car, took me with her, and we went downtown to the Safeway store at 308 Lakeside Avenue. The store was busy, the clerk was harried, and maybe I was a distraction too because I didn't like to wait in line. At any rate, when we got back into the car, Aunt Doris was laughing and saying things like, "Oh boy, yahoo, and what a lucky day!" The clerk had forgotten to take her sugar coupon, and that meant an extra ten pounds of sugar was now available. Money became secondary in importance to the coupons.

Tires were almost impossible to buy and people ran their tires completely bald until they blew out. Abandoned cars were common. A blown tire with no spare meant you left the car and walked home.

We had some hardworking neighbors, Jess and Essie Booher. They, with their four daughters, Gladys, Flavia, Eloise and Georgia, lived across the alley and east one lot at 319 N. 16th Street. Jess built a large chicken coop that could accommodate about one hundred chickens and they went into the egg business. They had a beautiful garden and flowerbeds plus a lawnmower that cut the grass real short and left a little wave in the lawn; it looked so tidy and I remember admiring their yard.

Jess was an enterprising fellow. He was a small man with a gimpy leg; he limped pretty badly, but he never seemed to stop working and he liked to dance at the country dances. He drove around in a stake-truck that always had empty barrels rattling around in the back. A stake-truck had a flatbed framed with upright stakes which had boards nailed horizontally to them to form an enclosure around the load. Certain days, he somehow had access to gasoline; so on those days the barrels weren't empty after all. He put the truck in his garage and closed the door every night, so the place always looked the same as nightfall arrived.

The Model A would be sitting in our garage with only enough gas in the tank to get Dad to his job at the Winton Sawmill in the community of Gibbs near the west edge of Coeur d'Alene on the Spokane River. He shared a ride with several other men, and only ran the car on the days when his turn came up.

On certain dark evenings there would be a tap-tap on our back door. I never did see an identifiable person, just a dim shadow who whispered, "Jess has gas tonight," and silently disappeared.

Dad's eyes would light up and Mom would get all cheery. Dad would put on his darkest clothes, slip out, grab an old water pail off the back porch and disappear. Sometimes Ralph and I turned off our bedroom light and, after our eyes adjusted, we could see that the alley was busy with silhouettes moving silently back and forth. Dad, and most of the men, carried the gas in water pails and used a large funnel to pour it into their cars. Gas was about 25 cents a gallon at the gas station when you could get it. I have no idea what the price was at Boohers'.

Most men smoked in those days, and now I sometimes wonder how we managed to avoid losing the whole neighborhood in a flash fire. It was a win-win situation for Jess. He spent a pleasant evening visiting and providing a favor for his friends and neighbors and made a few bucks besides.

Dad would return after an hour or so and say, "We have enough gas to go to Rose Lake and visit John and Mildred," or perhaps he would tell us, "We have enough to go to Spokane and visit Oscar and Ena and Gordon and Anna."

Then one night Jess sold everybody the wrong fuel. He mistakenly got a barrel of diesel or kerosene and our next car trip didn't last very long. The car started backfiring and clouds of black smoke poured out the exhaust pipe. Death of the engine was imminent. Some kind soul towed us home and helped Dad push the car into the garage.

So Dad rigged up a block and tackle in our garage and pulled the motor. I can't remember who came and helped him, but he had it overhauled after several weeks of trying to get parts. It was an expensive lesson, and he was less enthusiastic about buying gas at Boohers' garage after that.

In 1943 Dad was working at the Winton Mill for 65 cents an hour. That spring there were suddenly hundreds of jobs available for carpenters at Farragut Naval Base, a huge complex being built on the shores of Pend O'reille Lake near the small town of Bayview, to eventually train 294,000 sailors for war duty. Farragut was about twenty-five miles northeast of Coeur d'Alene. Dad had a collection of carpenter tools and knew how to use them. He had built our two-story garage and woodshed, plus the fancy outhouse, so was confident with his carpentry skills.

After a long discussion with Mom he decided to use enough gas to drive out to Farragut and inquire about a job. He was hired immediately and hurried home with the big news.

"I got hired," he exclaimed excitedly, "and they are paying $1.00 an hour!"

"We'll be rich!" Mom exclaimed. That wage for carpenters and laborers in North Idaho was unprecedented in those times.

He quickly built a 32-inch by 8-inch by 12-inch-deep wooden toolbox to carry his tools and was ready for action. He told us later that some of the "carpenters" showed up at Farragut with an armload of tools still wrapped with paper and string, straight from the hardware store. Big gray buses traveled between downtown Coeur d'Alene and Farragut every fifteen minutes, so he had a way to get to and from work. His sawmill days were over and this was a good thing because the screaming saws were destroying his hearing.

These were terrible times for many families, but Coeur d'Alene boomed as never before. Housing became critically short as wives and girlfriends followed their sailors to North Idaho. New apartments were slapped together in long barrack-like buildings at a place called Mullan Park, now known as McEuen Field. One of our neighbors built a dinky little cabin in his backyard with scrap lumber salvaged from the mill where he worked. He rented it continuously for the duration of the war.

People sometimes stopped and asked Dad if they could rent our garage. It had a dirt floor and no plumbing. No problem, some said—broken-down boxes and old boards would fix that. There was an ancient heating stove with a stovepipe sticking through a broken windowpane. That was good enough, they said. He was tempted, but didn't rent it. He was afraid somebody trying to keep warm would burn the place down.

Downtown Coeur d'Alene had about a dozen taverns in a four-block stretch of Sherman Avenue and they were overflowing every night of the week. The five movie theaters, Wilma, Dream, Liberty, Roxy and Little Roxy, were filled to capacity and

Typical wartime street scene. Sailor and woman crossing Sherman Avenue at 2nd Street with Wilma Theater on the left and Dream Theatre on the right. Museum of North Idaho photo.

the sidewalks teemed with sailors.

Red lights hung in the windows of numerous houses, including the houses on both sides of us for a while. The woman who lived to the east of us would walk down to the 1210 Tavern, and soon return with a man. She had a nice little setup on part of her back porch. I was too young to comprehend what was happening, but my little ears were always listening.

Well-established businesses had volume like they had never dreamed of. The Post Office stayed open until 8 pm so sailors could buy money orders. This bonanza wasn't good enough for one grocer, who found a way to exploit a good thing even further. He set a nice new broom beside the cash register, and if he knew the customer, nothing happened. If the customer was a stranger, he slipped in the price of the broom somewhere along the way. If he got caught, he apologized profusely.

"Oh, my goodness, I am really sorry," he'd say. "I could have sworn you set that broom there," and then he deducted the price from their total. Most didn't notice, and he took in a little extra each week selling one broom that never left the store.

The Coeur d'Alene Civic Center was built in the City Park in 1937 by twenty-seven WPA (Work Projects Administration) workers and was the source of much community pride. It was the largest log structure in the Northwest, measuring 138 by 136 feet. This one-of-a-kind building was built with Douglas fir and Tamarack logs, 24,903 linear feet of them, carefully selected from the forest for miles around. Logs forty to fifty feet long with virtually no taper were hard to find even in those days.

Soon after training was underway at Farragut, this large beautiful building was converted to a USO (United Service Organization) to be a comfortable place for lonely sailors who didn't care to frequent the taverns. Hundreds of Coeur d'Alene

Dream Theatre ca. 1945, 214 Sherman Avenue. Museum of North Idaho photo.

residents volunteered to entertain the sailors. Dance bands provided music every night with snacks and soft drinks always available.

One evening in October 1945, a sailor from New Jersey with pyromaniac tendencies hid in the building until it was closed. After everyone left he set a fire and crawled out a window. When the firemen arrived he helped them fight the fire with such frenzy

USO Building in Coeur d'Alene City Park. Museum of North Idaho photo.

that they became suspicious of him and started asking questions. He admitted what he had done, but that did nothing to replace this unique building since suitable logs simply were no longer to be found. It was a devastating loss for the citizens of Coeur d'Alene.

In July 1943 when I was six years old, a neighbor girl, Esther Lee Harkleroad, and I decided to take off and go exploring without telling our mothers. We walked to 18th Street and turned south to Sherman Avenue, which was also US Highway 10 in those years. We knew this was a dangerous street, and we held hands as we ran across really fast. We continued south on 18th for about five blocks to Lakeview Hill and followed a narrow little path to the top of the hill, exploring excitedly as we went along. From the top we could see a large body of water extending to a distant shoreline and tree-covered mountains. We talked it over, and determined this must be the Pacific Ocean we had been hearing so much about. As for the land we could see way over there beyond the water, well, that just had to be Japan.

We decided we had gone far enough for one day, and since we were getting hungry, we turned around and retraced the path down to 18th Street. As we came off Lakeview Hill a man stopped us and asked if we were lost.

"Oh no," I told him, "We're on our way home from Japan." He frowned and shook his head, but didn't ask any more questions. I noticed he kept watching us as we made our way north on 18th.

As Esther Lee and I approached our homes we noticed that there seemed to be an unusual number of people outside running around our neighborhood. Yep, you

From left, Esther Lee Harkleroad, Larry Strobel, Patty Blair and Richie Blair in 1943. Note vent for outhouse built into corner of woodshed/garage.

guessed it! They were looking for us. This situation parlayed into the worst spanking I had ever had, and I was forbidden to play with Esther Lee for a whole week.

I couldn't understand what all the excitement was about; I knew where we were all the time and besides, none of my friends, even Jim Abbott who got to go a lot of places, had been to Japan.

We were poor, but I didn't know it. Our life seemed fine to me. Many of our neighbors did not have cars, but we had our Model A Ford that ran quite a bit of the time when we had any gas.

One day Aunt Doris was at our house, and for reasons I can't remember, it became urgent that a message be taken to Uncle Jasper's and Aunt Ruth's ranch about two miles east of town. None of us had a telephone, Dad was at work, and Mom didn't know how to drive. So Aunt Doris said she would just take our car and go. She took me with her, and I thought that was great—she was fun.

We took care of business and started home. As we approached the east city limits she suddenly swerved off the road into a little open place in the woods near the western edge of Fernan Lake.

"Sorry," she said, "but we have to walk from here."

We started walking on streets I didn't recognize as we cut through some woods on little paths, and my legs were getting tired. Finally, after what seemed a very long time, we arrived home.

Pretty soon Dad came home from work, and Aunt Doris told him she had left our car at Fernan because she had looked ahead and the police were stopping every car. She knew they were checking for drivers' licenses and she had never bothered to buy one.

He thought this was hilarious, and he was "har, harring," all over the place.

"Earl," she said sweetly, "why don't you laugh while you walk, because that is the only way you are going to get your car home."

When Mom needed to call someone she would walk to the Barber's house two blocks away. Often she didn't have time to do that, so she wrote a note to Vera Barber and I would deliver it. Mrs. Barber would make the phone call for her and then write a note for me to take home.

We did have running water—cold only. Hot water was heated as needed in large pans and kettles on our wood-burning cook stove. We used lots of hot water for the Saturday night baths that took place in a large washtub placed on the kitchen floor. Ralph and I had to use the same water and took turns being first.

Monday was washday. The washing machine was stored on the back porch and was rolled on its casters into the kitchen to join three washtubs already set up on benches. Heated water was poured with soap powder into an electric washing machine that had a genuine gyrator to beat the dirt out of the clothes. Clothes were lifted out of the hot soapy water with a long-handled fork-like tool and run through a hand-cranked wringer into a washtub of lukewarm water, then stirred around to rinse out the soap. The wringer was on a swivel so it could be turned. The clothes were run through it again into a tub of cooler water. Here they were stirred some more (swivel that wringer again), and wrung once more into a tub of cold water. More stirring and supposedly the soap was rinsed out of the clothes well enough that it was time to wring them through the last time into a basket to be carried to the clothesline outside. Now the clothes had to be shaken out thoroughly and hung on the lines with clothespins. The housewife's prayer was for sunshine and a little breeze to dry the clothes before a rainstorm came along and also that no bird would fly over and drop a little bomb.

The final step was to empty the washtubs and washing machine. Mom emptied the tubs by dipping water with a pan into buckets that she carried outside and dumped. Then a garden hose was hooked to the washing machine and strung out to the driveway so the soapy water wouldn't kill the lawn. This was usually my after-school job. The wash water was way too much to pour into the sink because the cesspool would fill up too fast. Washday was a big deal with hours of hard work involved.

Mom's washday was always a lot more challenging if the weather was bad. Then the clothes had to be hung on the back porch and on a variety of clothes racks in our living room. When this happened our house smelled damp and the windows fogged over. Dad would fire up the wood-heating stove in the living room so the temperature would hit about eighty, and we felt like we were living in a sweat bath as we weaved our way between racks of drying clothes.

A full cesspool was a real source of irritation and meant a new one had to be dug immediately. It was usually dug quite close to the full one and a pipe was forced through the dirt to drain the overflow into the new hole. An average cesspool was about four to five feet deep and four to six feet across. Some yards had a long string of cesspools. The typical homeowner placed some old boards over the hole, threw a few inches of dirt on them and seeded it to grass. These boards were like a savings account for future trouble. Years later some poor fellow innocently mowing his lawn would suddenly crash through rotten boards and end up floundering in an old cesspool. I remember when this happened to our next-door neighbor, Mr. Thorsness. It was an unpleasant surprise for him and unexpected entertainment for the neighborhood as he cursed and waved his arms wildly as he struggled to climb out. Several neighbors did run over to assist and he wasn't hurt, just mad.

We had an icebox on the back porch and bought forty-pound blocks of ice at Valley Ice and Fuel, 11th and Mullan, or from Jim Prosser who delivered ice with a big blue and white truck. He carried the ice blocks on his shoulder with ice tongs and his shirt was always wet. We kids thought it was great sport to jump up on the back of his truck to get chips of ice to suck on. The real trick was to grab some ice and run before he came back and chased us away.

We were fortunate to have electricity. Our house had not been wired for wall switches or outlets so the lights hung on electric cords suspended from the ceiling. Above those swinging and swaying light bulbs there was a little black switch on each socket that had to turn one-half turn to light the bulb. To locate a switch in the dark was tricky and often involved kicking and/or falling over furniture while searching for that elusive hanging bulb that seemed to move as soon as it got dark.

We usually didn't lock our house, but we could lock it with a passkey. These

Edith Hamby Stowe and Floyd Stowe, ca. 1930. Photo courtesy of Ann Stowe Jordon.

Annaree and Albert Stowe ca. 1939. Photo courtesy of Ann Stowe Jordon.

wonderful keys, also called skeleton keys, were capable of opening multiple simple locks, so locking the door was a study in futility. As if that wasn't bad enough, Dad and Mom were always afraid of losing the key, so they "hid" it under a stick of wood on the porch windowsill. It really didn't matter—nobody ever broke into our house or any other house in the neighborhood that I can remember. Burglary was rare, with respect for other people's property pretty much a given.

Uncle Floyd and Aunt Edith with their two children, Floyd Jr., usually called Albert, and Anna Marie, lived six blocks east of our house at 2021 Coeur d'Alene Avenue. Uncle Floyd was a typical Stowe and raised a large garden along with raspberry bushes, a strawberry patch and fruit trees. Our neighborhood was still semi-rural and they had a red barn housing a milk cow, chickens and a couple pigs. Uncle Floyd had married Edith Hamby in 1930. She was an excellent seamstress, worked hard in the garden, and canned hundreds of jars of vegetables and fruits each season. She even milked the cow when Floyd wasn't home. Uncle Floyd (often called Shorty) worked at the Winton Mill with Dad until about 1940 when he landed a job with a line crew at our local electrical utility, Washington Water Power Co. (now Avista). This was steady, good-paying work that lasted twelve months a year.

Anna Marie was two years older than I, but she and I were frequent playmates. Anna Marie was too much for us kids to pronounce, so we shortened it to Annaree; pretty soon everyone was calling her by that name. I liked going to their house and she took the lead when we explored the woods beyond their property. We were fascinated by French Gulch Creek which flowed out of French Gulch and wound its way through the woods where Fernan Elementary would be constructed many years later. We raced "boats," sticks and pieces of wood, and fortunately never fell into the fast-running water.

Occasionally we had a Sunday family reunion at their house and the front yard became a baseball field. The cousins played along with the adults, and it was great fun until somebody overran first base and plowed into Aunt Edith's flowers. Then she would come out and say, "No more of that," and we had to calm the game down a little.

One of Mom's best friends was Beulah Masten. Laura Jean, their oldest daughter, was almost exactly my age and she was one of my earliest friends. A visit to their house was always enjoyable, and if Laura's dad, Wesley, was home we would coax him to play their piano for us. He played professionally and was quite a showman.

I remember those warm sunny summer days when, after lunch, Mom would say "Let's walk down to Mastens'." They lived at 402 S. 16th Street. The seven-block walk would be pleasant and we always walked slowly admiring the yards and gardens. Some of the best times were when we walked from Mastens' to S. 19th and onto the trail around Lakeview Hill. The trail was adjacent to the Potlatch Forest Mill and the sights, sounds and smells of that busy complex were interesting and agreeable. It seemed comforting to hear the mill whistle several times a day, knowing men were at work to support their families and all was well. The timber industry was what Coeur d'Alene was really all about in those years.

For me, the highlight of the walk was the remains of an old steamboat abandoned slightly east of the big rock that marked the eastern end of Sanders Beach. It was one of the last of the big boats that cruised on the lake for so many years. Most of the boats retired over the years were burned to the waterline and sunk. This beautiful boat, The *Miss Spokane*, had been run aground in the 1930s and left as a monument of sorts to the glory days of the big boats. It had been a poorly designed boat for Coeur d'Alene Lake, as the main deck was too high for the docks and loading and unloading was a problem.

Miss Spokane steamboat abandoned at east end of Sanders Beach; buffeted by the elements until being dismantled during low-water winter of 1954-1955. Museum of North Idaho photo.

Miss Spokane was a landmark to be anticipated each time we walked the trail. It seemed huge to me, especially when the water was low and most of the hull, the decks and super structure were visible. In the mid-1940s it still looked pretty good, but the sunshine and waves were taking their toll. During periods of high water most of the boat would disappear and the waves and wind would wreak havoc with the super-structure.

Some days we walked through the neighborhood to the former sawmill property at the foot of S.11th Street. This location was now the site of a fish hatchery. The men who ran the hatchery were pleasant and friendly and always gave us a tour so we could look at the fish. There were ponds and pools and troughs with fingerlings to fish several inches long. After the hatchery was moved, this area was converted to Ray Jones Boat Works.

These walking visits were a happy part of my childhood. We had no television sets or video games to keep us occupied and it was a good time to grow up as we invented our own fun and games. There were no organized leagues for youngsters and we enthusiastically organized neighborhood games of kickball, softball, hopscotch, jump rope, Annie Annie Over and hide and seek.

I started first grade at Harding Elementary School, 411 North 15th Street, in

September 1943. My teacher was Mrs. Fisher, and her husband was an officer at Farragut Naval Station. It only took a few weeks for our room to become the envy of the school. Candy bars were rarely available at the civilian stores, but they were readily available at Farragut. Mr. Fisher would bring home a supply, usually Hershey Bars, and Mrs. Fisher would bring some to school on special days or Fridays. She would break the bars into small pieces or squares, and we would each get one or two. Boy, that was the best tasting food in the world! I would take a tiny nibble and savor the flavor as long as possible. Some of the older kids were downright jealous when they found out. We should have kept our mouths shut.

Mrs. Fisher started a rhythm band with the second grade room included. She had a collection of small drums, sticks, castanets, wood blocks, plus various doodads that could be shaken, rattled, or hit. This was my first experience with an organized musical group. I learned to count and play rhythm with others—it was great fun.

During this first year of school was when I met some of my best longtime friends. I already knew Jim Abbott and Laura Masten as they were family friends. Jean Ross, Gene Branson, Jean Olson, Diane Lavonture, Joan Leonard, Bob Boughton, Donna Pieratt, Violet Miller, Virginia Monson, Jim Clouse, and Kay Osborne are friends I have had for over sixty-five years. Some of these "Harding kids" I still see regularly. Even if we don't meet often, we are instantly comfortable when we do get together. You just can't beat this kind of golden friendship.

Ernie Cook was one of my very best first-grade friends. We played together frequently before and after school. He lived with his family at 2001 Lakeside Avenue. His seventh birthday was my first experience with a surprise party. At the appropriate time his mother sent him to get some items at the Wayside Grocery six blocks away. That gave his friends and classmates time to arrive at the Cook home and hide behind chairs and a sofa. When he came through the door we jumped up and yelled "Happy Birthday!" His eyes sort of glazed over and he stood staring in disbelief. There is just nothing like a well-done surprise party. It turned out to be one of the happiest days of his young life and, as I look back, this was extremely important. The next fall school was barely underway when Ernie didn't show up for class. Then we heard he was sick from a bad toothache, but nobody thought too much about it. A few days later our teacher, Miss Dewald, had the sad task of telling us that Ernie had died from an abscessed tooth. I still feel a great sadness about his death.

During first grade Thanksgiving vacation Violet Miller and her family went out of town to visit relatives. She had the misfortune of being exposed to chickenpox while she was visiting, and came down with them after she got home, exposed all her friends, and I had to miss my first grade Christmas party because of Violet. But, then, so did a bunch of other kids. By Christmas time Harding School was pretty much a brick ghost town as this miserable, itchy disease roared through the school.

Schools were involved with paper drives as part of the community effort to support the war. Students were expected to bring all available newspapers from home and whatever they could collect from neighbors. On designated days we took these papers to school, usually with the help of a parent, and piled them in the hall. Jim Abbott had a good-sized wagon, and I remember him pulling it into the schoolyard with a tremendous load. He was the champion paper gatherer. Jim showed leadership abilities even at this early age and has been a "take charge" guy as long as I have known him.

On designated days there were parades to promote the collection and salvage of scrap iron. Many farmers and loggers used this as an incentive to clean up forty or fifty years' worth of discarded tools, implements and trucks—you name it. There were some terrific truckloads of all shapes and sizes of rusty iron as patriotism reached a feverish height.

Some nights we had Air Raid practice. It was well-publicized so there was no excuse for not knowing about it. The plan was to darken the town so if Japanese planes flew over, there would be no lights to indicate a town existed below them.

At the appointed time the air-raid siren on the city hall blew for several minutes, and then all lights were to be off, shades drawn, street lights off, and all traffic stopped. Every neighborhood had a patrol person who roamed an assigned area, and if any light was visible, it brought a knock on the door with an order to turn it off. We huddled in our living room, shades drawn, with a dim flashlight available if we happened to need to see where we were going during the practice. Sometimes Dad slipped out to look around and, sure enough, it was black everywhere. The Japanese planes never came, but the town was prepared. Frankly, I think it was just another way to remind us the USA was at war.

Mrs. Fisher was a dedicated and thoughtful teacher, and I give her full credit for getting me off to a successful start with reading, writing, arithmetic and music.

My grandma, Flora Stowe, died at home on April 27, 1944 after a long illness. I was too young to be allowed to attend the funeral. All the younger cousins came to our house and we had a quiet time together while our parents were at the service.

During the summer between first and second grade the Presbyterian Church at 6th and Lakeside had a two-week Summer Bible School (kind of like Sunday school on weekdays). Mom and Jim Abbott's mother, Grace, decided Jim and I should attend. They took us the first day, got us signed up, and then we were on our own.

We would meet at one of our homes each morning and ride our tricycles the twelve blocks to the church. Nobody seemed to think there was anything unusual for two seven-year-olds to be crossing streets and weaving through traffic on tricycles. That should give us all a clue about how scarce traffic actually was and how slow it moved in the 1940s.

One day on our way home, the cotter pin holding the right rear wheel on my tricycle broke and the wheel fell off. Jim took charge of the situation, told me to ride his trike, and he would wheel my broken-down equipment home for me. His tricycle was bigger than mine, and I got going way too fast on the little hill between 11th and 12th on Sherman. I couldn't stop so I drove off the sidewalk into a yard and tipped over. I scraped up my right arm, and was crying because I was hurt. Poor Jim! His day had really come unraveled. He eventually got me home, and I remember how relieved he looked as he went pedaling off for home. Even at that age I was impressed with a friend who would not abandon me and do whatever it took to get me home.

My second grade teacher was Miss Jeanette Dewald. She wasn't nearly as patient as Mrs. Fisher. She was demanding and strict which was okay with me because I didn't have any trouble learning. The kids who were inattentive or mischievous

Flora Kinney Stowe's funeral May 1, 1944. Front: George Stowe and Gordon. Back: Doris, Ena, Ruth, Bryan, Beulah and Floyd.

ran head-on into her impatience. If she became unhappy with a student, she started picking on him and, unfair as it was, he was in for a miserable year. One lad who had problems was Dick Bitterman. No wonder he didn't learn—he was sitting out in the hall half the time for some infraction or other. I enjoyed Dick's company and we often shot marbles together after school. The running war between them made me feel uncomfortable and I felt sorry for Dick.

One spring day Dick decided it was time to attempt a truce—bury the hatchet, so to speak. He showed up at school with a nice bouquet of daffodils, and presented them to Miss Dewald. She was impressed, and praised him for his thoughtfulness as she arranged them in a big vase on her desk. This was looking like a brilliant maneuver on the part of Dick as Miss Dewald relaxed, and was downright pleasant. As we began the day's lessons we were about fifteen minutes into the school day when the school principal, Miss Gretchen Brautigam, jerked the door open and came storming in.

"Ah ha," she snapped at Miss Dewald, "Where did the daffodils come from?"

"Why, Dick brought them for me," she answered. "Wasn't that the nicest thing?"

"Maybe so and maybe not," said Miss Brautigam. "I just got a phone call from a woman down on Front Avenue who saw a young boy pick her daffodils and then run away."

"Where did you get the flowers, Dick?" asked Miss Dewald.

"We raise them in our yard," was the answer.

Then Dick's next-door neighbor girl was queried about the growing of daffodils in the Bitterman yard.

"No, they don't have any," she said.

"Did I say our yard?" said Dick. "I meant my grandmother's yard."

Well, one of the other kids lived next door to his grandma, and here again there was no recollection of daffodils growing in her yard either.

"She, uh, grows them in her basement," was Dick's next attempt.

Miss Brautigam was a severe-looking woman with her hair pulled back in a bun. She didn't spend much time smiling on a good day, and now she was downright cranky. She practically emitted sparks as she grabbed Dick by the collar and whisked him and the ill-advised bouquet out the door. We didn't see him again until after lunch and the daffodils didn't come back at all. He had the right idea—wrong method.

Dick wasn't the only student who took his lumps from Miss Dewald. I had some rough days with her myself. I had a favorite marble that was slightly bigger than the others and very pretty. This was my "shooter." One day when I was bored I took it out of my pocket, and was rolling it around on my desk. It fell on the floor and she was on me like a cat. I had dropped a marble on the floor and her rule was that any marble landing on the floor was hers.

I tried to make a quick switch, but she caught me, and demanded the marble that fell on the floor. I was so desperate to get my lucky shooter back that I hung around after school and begged her to give it to me. No dice, I never did get it back. I couldn't think of any reason she would want marbles. I never once saw her shooting marbles with Miss Brautigam or any other teacher.

I still wonder what she did with my precious marble.

Most people had wood-burning stoves, and all but the poorly organized folks planned ahead carefully so that a supply of dry wood was always available. Dad talked with disdain about people who tried to dry wood in the oven shortly before tossing it into the firebox. Several wood companies delivered cords of slab wood cut into sixteen-inch lengths. These entrepreneurs of the day contracted to buy the slabs from the sawmill, thus saving them from the mill's teepee burner. We bought ours from our neighbor, Ray Bjornstad. The cost was five dollars per load, and dry, planed board ends (trim) were also available to be used for kindling or quick fires.

Dad taught me how to pile the wet slab wood we bought early each spring into rows that were loosely stacked, bark down, so it would dry by fall. Flat surfaces were never placed together because the wood would mold and wouldn't dry well. He also started teaching me how to use an axe and hatchet to split wood and kindling. This was a year-round job because of the cook stove and the hottest day of summer was no exception. The fire had to be blazing away to cook, bake and heat water. If it happened to be a day for canning fruit or vegetables the kitchen was sweltering all day. Sometimes we moved the kitchen table and chairs outside for dinner to escape the over-heated kitchen.

One bath per week was about as good as it got, and Right Guard hadn't been invented yet. I now wonder how we stood each other. I guess everyone had the same problem, and some of the men who worked at a mill always smelled like wet sawdust.

The summer of 1944, when I was seven, we had company. Aunt Alma came from Petaluma, California in her 1942 Chevrolet she had bought just before all the car factories were converted to make military vehicles. I don't know how she managed to get enough gas to travel that far; perhaps it was classed as a business trip. She owned a medical laboratory that was years ahead of any facility in the Coeur d'Alene area. At any rate, the neighbors kept coming over to inspect this new car. A 1942 model was and is a real rarity.

She was really nice, and we boys loved having her at our house. One afternoon I started hearing phrases like, "Let's eat out," and, "We could go out for dinner," and "Where's a good place to eat?" Ralph and I were completely confused by these remarks. We always ate at home except for the occasional Sunday when we ate at the home of one of our relatives or friends, like the George Armstrongs who had the cherry orchard on Armstrong Hill. When we did that, Mom always helped with the cooking.

This day would be different. We all rode downtown in Aunt Alma's wonderful car, and parked in front of Elizabeth Ann's Tea Room at 406 Lakeside Avenue. Mark and Elizabeth Ann Anderson were both superior cooks and had built a popular restaurant there. Part of the property featured outside tables surrounded by a latticework of walls and a roof covered by vines. Colored lights strung on the walls and ceiling gave this outside area a festive appearance. Our family had never been here or any other restaurant.

We went inside and a lady took us to a table to be seated. Ralph and I were really perplexed. There were people coming and going and eating at other tables and we didn't know any of them. The next thing we knew, Aunt Alma was discussing food with Mom and Dad as she studied a piece of paper. Then a different lady came and asked us what we wanted to eat. Well now, this was just amazing. She left, and Mom just sat there.

Ralph whispered to me, "How can we get anything to eat? Mom is just sitting here."

"I don't know," I whispered back, "We will have to wait and see. She will probably go and cook something as soon as she gets done talking to Aunt Alma."

She didn't budge, and pretty soon the second lady came back with a tray of plates with food on them. Now we were really baffled. The food smelled and tasted great, so we quit worrying and started eating. Then she showed up with a glass of milk for each of us. How had she known we wanted that? Ralph was on such good behavior that he didn't even spill any of his, a habit he was famous for. It was a wonderful evening as far as I was concerned.

It was a long time before we ate out again. I can't remember any of our friends going out to eat except on very special occasions.

We had several interesting neighbors. Across 15th Street to the west was the Swans' house, and next to them were Caryls. Mrs. Caryl was a real talker, and was an expert in the art of burying her listener in never-ending detail. To say she murdered the King's English would be an understatement. Mrs. Swan, on the other hand, could one-up Mrs. Caryl on that score, as she completely laid the English language to total ruin. She couldn't talk as fast as Mrs. Caryl, but she probably hadn't gotten a verb tense right in years, said "ain't" frequently, talked through her nose, and had no family secrets. None of the other neighbors had any secrets either when she got done.

Ralph and I learned early on that these two were real entertaining, but Mom would usually suggest we play outside as soon as she saw one of them coming. If we saw company coming first, we learned to quietly hide in our bedroom and listen. Sometimes though we would start laughing too loud and get exiled to the back yard. This went on for years. When these two showed up together, we knew it was big—usually an upcoming divorce or a pregnant neighbor girl. Both their husbands had drinking problems, and I eventually figured out why. Of course, that caused more problems, and Mrs. Swan carried on something terrible because her husband "came home drunk as a skunk and couldn't go to work."

Downtown there were those old men who sat on benches here and there on Sherman Avenue. Mom eyed them warily, and we gave them a wide berth when we went to shop at the Buster Brown Shoe Store, Montgomery Wards, JC Penney's or Woolworth's—everybody's favorite. We had to walk on the edge of the sidewalk to avoid the men who spat tobacco juice on the sidewalk, wore long overcoats with inside pockets that "probably" contained bottles of whiskey or playing cards or pictures of unclad girls (according to my mother). They hung out in the taverns, but they didn't look dangerous to me as they leaned on their canes and smiled.

Mrs. Caryl said at least some of those old coots told dirty stories and "baited" unsuspecting tourists. They were always a wealth of information, she said, and if the subject of population came up one of them would always have an exact number at the ready—say 9,457.

"How do you know that to be the exact number?" would be the automatic question.

"That's easy—it's been the same for years now."

"How can that be possible?" (It's just too easy.)

"Why, because, every time a baby is born somebody skips town." The men laughed, but "ladies" like Mrs. Caryl were offended.

I never got acquainted with any of these "interesting" old guys in my early years, and frankly, Mom was probably right—no desirable education there.

Our neighbors across the street, Clinton and Irene Blair, were good friends, and Ralph and I played with their children, Patty and Ritchie. In early 1944 Clinton got a civilian job at Farragut, and to avoid travel expenses each day he was allowed to move his family into an apartment complex on base.

One Sunday we had enough gas, thanks to Jess, to drive out and visit them. It

Entrance to Farragut Naval Station. Museum of North Idaho photo.

was great to see Patty and Ritchie again, and we were having a super-good time playing in the yard. One of Ritchie's newest "toys" was a bow and arrow. I didn't have anything like that, and found them rather intriguing. I couldn't get the arrow to stick in anything, but then I noticed Blairs' downstairs neighbors had some washing hanging on the clothesline, and I idly wondered if that arrow could possibly penetrate a sheet that was fluttering in the breeze. Sure enough, my aim was true, and it went through both sides of the sheet draped over the line and hung up about mid-arrow.

Having completed this experiment successfully, it belatedly occurred to me that since sheets were next to impossible to acquire in these war years, that this was most likely an ill-advised thing to have done.

Patty said, "You shouldn't have done that! I'm going upstairs and tell my dad!"

The arrow was stuck, so we abandoned it, took the rest of the toys, and ran upstairs to Blairs' apartment. Patty told her parents, and her dad ran over and looked out the window. Both sets of parents seemed to be experiencing sudden transformations. Clinton was bald with just a fringe of hair all around. His bald head was instantly very red. Irene's dark complexion (she was part Native American), lightened up considerably. Mom's face looked downright chalky, and I could see that Dad was wanting to laugh as that arrow waggled around while the sheet blew in the breeze. A guffaw would have been terribly inappropriate, so he managed to take on a very stern look. My fanny began to sting in anticipation.

Before any of them could think of a plan to escape this unexpected bit of trouble, the downstairs neighbors sauntered out to collect their dry laundry. The man began yelling and shouting words Mom didn't want us to hear and forbade us to use.

Clinton made a snap decision and shoved all four of us into the closet. He threatened us with all sorts of misfortune if we made even a tiny noise. The knock on the door came, of course, within a very few minutes. There were never four north Idaho kids any quieter or more scared than we were as we cowered in that stuffy closet among the hanging clothes. Of course, we all suddenly remembered we hadn't gone to the bathroom lately. We could hear Clinton as he denied having any children. His company from town had no children either and he hadn't seen any children playing outside. The sheet owner was furious and he didn't leave for what seemed like an eternity. In regular times Clinton would have apologized and bought him a new sheet, but none was available. We had to play quietly inside the rest of the day, and we didn't go home until we could exit under cover of darkness. Patty was furious with me and I was miserable. This was the biggest trouble I had been in since Esther Lee and I made our visit to Japan.

My third grade year was a memorable time because World War II came to an end on V-J Day, August 14, 1945. The church bells rang and the sirens downtown blew for hours. Everywhere people were in the streets laughing, crying, yelling and hugging. Anybody with liquor drank it and shared with friends. It was, indeed, a wonderful time except for the families who had lost men in the conflict. Some of our friends and neighbors would never be the same and I hated the war. Our family was lucky; we only lost one—my cousin Glenn Stowe.

This was the year the school nurse discovered I had poor eyesight. My teacher, Eloise Scheetz, a soft-spoken, kind and caring lady, had to seat me in the front row because I couldn't read the writing on the blackboard. I didn't know any better—I thought everyone saw like that.

There were no "real eye doctors" in Coeur d'Alene, only optometrists, so Dad decided we had better go to Spokane for an exam. Our car wasn't running very well at the time, so we rode on the Auto Interurban bus that made six trips a day to Spokane. I remember going into a very tall building and into a waiting room full of people. A

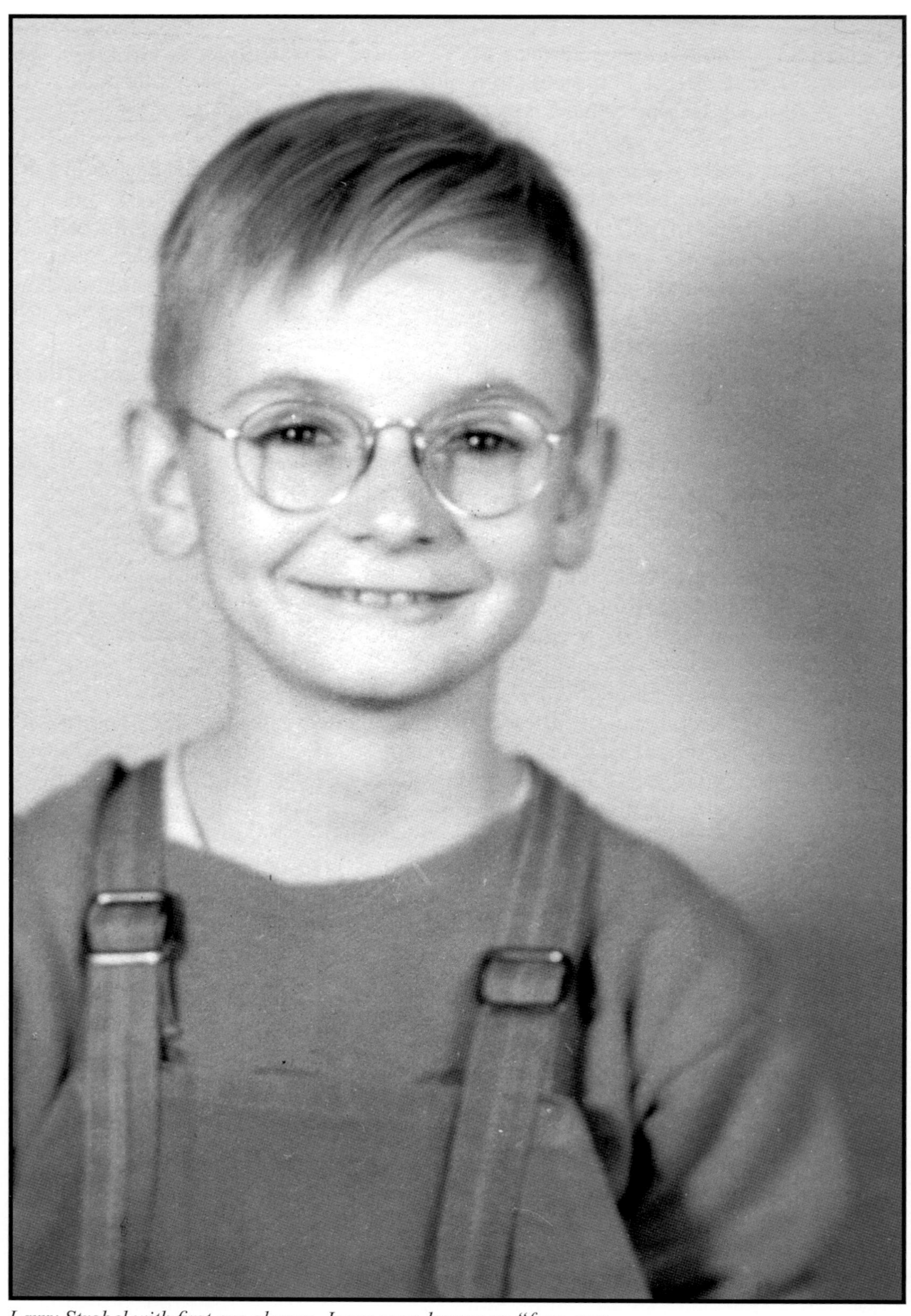

Larry Strobel with first eye glasses. I was soon known as "four-eyes.

nurse put drops into my eyes and it hurt. It was a lengthy exam, and we had to come back after lunch for more drops. Finally, late in the afternoon the doctor made his final evaluation and prescribed glasses. Then he told Dad as I sat there, "His eyes are weak, and as he gets older they will keep getting weaker until he is blind."

Strobel siblings in 1945. In front, Alma and Gladys. Earl and John are in back.

Now there is a bit of news every third-grader wants to hear, isn't it? Fortunately, the old doctor was wrong. My little wire-rimmed glasses were sure neat, and I could see things I didn't know existed. My eyes did slowly get weaker, but they were healthy. By age eighteen they stabilized and have changed very little since.

My Grandma Strobel, Celestia, died in Petaluma, California December 6, 1945. She had been living there with her daughter, Alma, for several years. Uncle John and Dad drove down for the service and had a nice reunion with their sisters, Alma and Gladys. She was buried at Forest Cemetery in Coeur d'Alene. Later George Strobel's remains were removed from Lane Cemetery and buried beside her.

Not long after the war ended the dismantling of Farragut began. Good Hope Wrecking Company, owned by Frank Wester, had the contract to move many of the buildings to Coeur d'Alene. Some of the two-story officers' quarters became some of the nicest homes in town: 419 South 17th, 1319 Ash, 414 North 17th, 622 North 19th and 1809 Boyd are some examples. He moved parts of several buildings to 1519 Sherman, took the roofs off half of them, lifted the other half on top of these with a crane, and made the two-story Portal Motel. This motel was later renamed the Budget Saver and lasted until 2001 when it was destroyed by fire.

The good news was that much-sought-after plumbing supplies were suddenly available via salvage at Farragut. Dad drove out there, bought a nice variety of pipe, elbows and tees, and started working to convert our pantry into a bathroom.

We had an old claw-foot bathtub that had been stored in our garage since 1940. Dad brought it into the ex-pantry and hooked it up. Then he bought a hot water tank, set it in the corner by the tub, ran water pipes through the wall and into the firebox of the cook stove. This was a clunky-looking arrangement, but it worked. That is, it worked as long as there was a fire in the stove. Now we had running hot water—sometimes.

The next big news was the toilet Dad bought and hooked up next to the bathtub. We were on a roll now. An indoor toilet was the envy of the neighborhood. However, before long the cesspool filled up and nothing in the house would drain. So we had to go with the backup system—the outhouse. Our cesspool was in the garden so Dad had to dig up part of the garden to add a new one.

Things only got better. The city sewer lines were extended into our neighborhood. This provided months of entertainment for us kids as the big "steam shovel" made its way along the various streets and alleys. The trench was eight to ten feet deep. Sometimes before the pipes could be lowered and cemented together, the sides of the ditch would cave in. One day a pipe layer was buried up to his neck, right behind Bartons' house at 1522 Coeur d'Alene Avenue. The workers dug him out and he was scared but not hurt. In some alleys buildings were built right to the edge of the alley on both sides and there was nowhere to pile dirt. The contractor brought in a long conveyer on wheels and backfilled the ditch with the freshly dug dirt as they went along. Some days the big shovel broke water mains, and that really made for an exciting day!

Dad was tired of digging cesspools and wanted to hook up to the sewer right away. I helped him dig the trench from our house to the alley. There went a section of the garden again. He bought eight-foot sections of a new invention called Orangeburg pipe. The sections were connected together by a sleeve that slid over both pipes and this theoretically kept out roots. Once the ditch was dug we could lay the pipe quickly. He went right through the cesspool with a length of pipe, and didn't take care to pack enough dirt under it as he bridged the hole. We got hooked up and everything was just great until the weight of the dirt broke the unsupported pipe. So now we were back to the outhouse and had to dig up the garden again.

The Farragut job ended before the war was over and Dad had returned to woods work. He was looking for a better job, and in early 1946, got his chance. It was announced that Kaiser Aluminum Company was going to build a huge new plant in the Spokane valley at Trentwood.

Dad had taken correspondence courses for several years to try and catch up on the education he had not received as a youngster. He would labor over papers many evenings and then proudly mail his completed work. He wrote a beautiful hand, conquered arithmetic, learned how to compose a business letter, fill out forms, how to use a dictionary, spell and use correct verb tenses.

Dad drove over to Trentwood to inquire about employment. Now his hard work paid off. In those days most men got hired because a friend or relative at the mill or mine put in a good word for them with the boss or foreman. When the applicant showed up, the foreman looked him over. If the guy appeared halfway healthy and strong, and "Joe" had said he was an okay worker, he was hired. A handshake was about all it took to seal the deal. Of course, they could be fired in a hurry too.

The folks at Kaiser had a new innovation called a job application. Some men had a tough time with these papers, but Dad had no problem. He gave them lots of information and spelled it right. He had some experience with electric motors at the sawmill, and impressed the Kaiser personnel people so much that he landed a one-of-a-kind job at the plant. He was hired to oil and maintain over three thousand electric motors in this sprawling complex, which had motors all the way from beneath the floor to the roof. Various motors required weekly, monthly, or semi-annual oiling. Every service had to be recorded in a ledger. This was an important job because a burned-out motor could stop production.

At last he had a job that lasted twelve months a year and provided benefits. The best part was—it was always the day shift. Almost every other job at Kaiser involved a shift change every two weeks. His badge number was 511, quite a low number for this facility. In his case it was true that life began at forty.

One thing that made Dad happy was his ability to help some of our friends and neighbors with business letters. These people were not dumb, just under-educated. Thanks to his correspondence course, Dad would listen to a friend's problem, draft an outline for him, and write a correctly spelled and punctuated letter in that big bold style he had. Then all the fellow had to do was sign the letter and drop it in the mail. We had some very pleased and relieved people walking out our door.

It was true that school wasn't considered very important by many members of my parents' generation. Many families were short of money and decided any boy fourteen or so was old enough to work full-time on the farm, in the woods, or to apprentice with a plumber, carpenter, or electrician, etc. Girls didn't need to go to school to learn how to cook, sew and change a baby.

Dad took Ralph and me fishing sometimes, usually at Fernan Lake. If we had enough money, he would rent a rowboat from Sam Theis. Sam had about a dozen brightly painted rowboats tied to the dock in front of his house on the shore of Fernan Lake at what is now 112 Hazelwood Drive. The old house is still occupied and in good repair.

We didn't have any real fishing poles, so Dad would stop somewhere on the way and select a nice straight stick out of a tall bush, take his knife, cut it, and strip off the branches. Then he'd tie some fishing line on one end, add some leader and a hook, install a bobber, and we were in business. With the worms we dug out of the garden our fishing equipment budget was almost zero.

Great Uncle Charlie Williams would occasionally talk Dad into taking him fishing with us boys. He loved to fish, and if he could talk someone into a fishing trip, he was just like a kid on the way to the candy store.

He took one look at our fishing poles and cringed. He didn't say much, but within a week he showed up at our house with two six-foot bamboo poles. They were painted dark green and equipped with small reels with plenty of extra line wound on them. These were for Ralph and me. They were nice poles with eyelets attached for the line to travel through and I eventually caught hundreds of fish with mine.

It was quite an adventure to fish with Charlie. For him I think the best part of the trip was the anticipation, and he would talk about going for days.

We would rent a boat from Sam and then the adventure started. Charlie's legs were pretty stove-up and his balance wasn't the best. To get off the dock into the boat was a challenge, and it was always a chore to keep him from falling into the lake and/or tipping the boat over. We'd get loaded up then Dad would row us across the lake to some likely looking spot while Charlie spun a few yarns about his past fishing exploits.

Dad would get worms on all the hooks, and get everybody set to fish. We would no more than get comfortable when Charlie would decide he needed to go to shore to relieve himself. Dad would sigh, pull in his line and row us to the closest little beach he could find; Charlie would rock the boat, almost fall overboard and get his feet wet getting out.

The next time he needed to go he told Dad, "Never mind rowing over to the shore. I will just stand up and pee over the side," in a voice loud enough to be heard for a mile across the water.

He rocked the boat, almost fell overboard and got his feet wet. No matter how we did it, the end result was unsatisfactory.

We usually managed to get home with some perch and sunfish and an occasional bass or crappie in the mix. Dad would end up cleaning all the fish while Charlie told some more stories. There was no way even my patient dad could stand a steady diet of fishing trips with Charlie.

These were the years Charlie and Grandpa Stowe were still feeling well and could accurately remember places, dates and events—or so they each claimed.

Some days they would both go for a walk and by chance end up in our living room telling stories. They would get into some great stories like the one about the supposedly dead deer that leaped to his feet, made good his escape, and scattered

Lizzie and Charles Williams at home, 614 N. 15th Street.

the hunters all over the landscape as they were preparing to skin him. The recurring problem was they could not agree which year each particular event took place. I never could see what difference it made, but they somehow thought it was of utmost importance.

"George, my dear fellow," Charlie would say with great conviction, "it was 1909 because of--," and he would cite some historical landmark. Charlie was tenacious when arguing, always in a loud voice, but it was important to him to come across as a polite English gentleman.

"Charlie, my good man," Grandpa would counter, "it was 1910 because—," here came some more historical facts and figures. Grandpa was polite in a soft-spoken, direct, factual, no-nonsense way that was intended to end the argument.

Sometimes the original story never did get finished, but we had the enjoyment of six or eight others as they argued about what year an event occurred.

Charlie got carried away with some real whoppers on occasion, and I knew he had gone beyond all reasonable basis of fact when Aunt Lizzie would yell, "CHAARLIEE!!!" from the kitchen.

Jim Abbott built a float on his wagon for the 4th of July Kiddie's Parade that summer of 1946. He talked Jean Ross into helping him; she was the princess on the wagon and he supplied the power. I didn't get involved with this escapade and I

Classmates Jim Abbott and Jean Ross set to participate in the 4th of July Kiddie's Parade.

Larry Strobel and Jim Abbott; birthday party at Coeur d'Alene City Park with Playland Pier in background.

understand they only tipped the wagon over once during a practice run.

My fourth grade year was a pleasant time, with teacher Alice Reis doing a nice job with us kids. She was calm and methodical, didn't pick on anybody and kept her class under control.

Something exciting always seemed to pop up for me. One day at afternoon recess, I was up to bat in the schoolyard softball game. I hit a foul ball that was a real screamer, and it headed right for Miss Brautigam's room. That ball must have had eyes because it picked out the center of a windowpane, and kept right on going. Splintered glass and the ball blew right past the desk where she was grading papers, and made it clear into the hallway. I didn't expect her to be laughing when she made it out to the schoolyard, and she wasn't. As I recall, that little stunt cost me 77 cents for a new pane, and I had to shake the coins out of my piggybank. The janitor was Mr. Treman and he replaced the windowpane. He was a kindly old gent who worked hard and he didn't bawl me out for making a mess. Arta Treman and his wife, Lulu, lived at 1724 Sherman Avenue and had beautiful flower gardens.

I had another baseball misadventure not long afterward. Aunt Doris and Cousin MaryLynn had come to live with us for a while because Aunt Doris was about seven months pregnant. Uncle John was traveling around the Northwest looking for a job, and a pregnant woman should be settled somewhere near a doctor and hospital. This arrangement suited me fine. Aunt Doris was fun, and Mom was more good-natured when she was with us. Why not? Aunt Doris did a lot of the cooking. Cousin MaryLynn was an agreeable playmate, although she palled around with Ralph more than with me because they were nearer the same age.

There was a movie that Mom and Aunt Doris really wanted to see, and they kept talking about going. Finally they each had saved up the required quarter plus a couple of dimes each to ride to and from downtown on the city bus. They were real excited, and asked Grandpa Stowe to come over and look after us kids while they went to the matinee. He was happy to come over—he had been pretty lonely after Grandma died in 1944.

I was playing around outside with my baseball bat and a softball. Grandpa was playing Chinese checkers with Ralph and MaryLynn inside. The two sisters came out to leave and were happy as a couple of schoolgirls taking off for an adventure. Meanwhile I was hitting the ball into the air, chasing it down and hitting it somewhere else. I guess it didn't take much to keep me entertained. The ladies stood on the corner and waited for the bus. I was across the street from them, and I hit the ball in their general direction. Keep in mind that I couldn't have hit the side of a barn if I had wanted to. This was a long, looping fly ball. As it descended I could see it was going to land somewhere close to the sisters. Neither moved nor put up a hand and I watched in horror as that ball hit Aunt Doris square in the stomach. She screamed and doubled over in pain just as the bus pulled up. They waved the bus on and slowly headed back to our house.

"You have killed the baby," Mom screamed at me.

Aunt Doris lay down on our sofa and she looked real sick. Of course Mom was really yelling at me. Usually she was quick to administer a spanking, but this was so serious that my punishment would be meted out when Dad got home from work.

This had to be the low point of my life so far. If there was ever a nine-year-old who felt worse than I did that day, I don't know who it was. I was sick with fright and worry. Aunt Doris was one of my favorite people.

Finally Dad came home, and Mom immediately demanded that he and I adjourn to the woodshed where I was to receive the beating of my life.

He sat down on the chopping block.

"Tell me what happened," he said wearily.

I was crying hysterically, but he finally got the details out of me. He had been sitting there with a piece of kindling wood in his hand and now he tossed it over his shoulder.

"I know you didn't do this on purpose," he said. "I think you have suffered enough and I am not going to spank you for an accident. However, don't you ever dare tell your mother!" This was a secret that was forever kept.

Now the waiting began. Would the baby be born dead? Would the baby be an idiot? Would Aunt Doris be all right? This was a heavy load to carry around, and I worried endlessly.

The next week Uncle John showed up in a wheezing old International pickup pulling a trailer and they left for a new job in Glendive, Montana.

Finally on February 3rd, 1947 we got the good news. Janis Ardell Gammel had arrived and everything was fine. The heavy load was lifted and I was flooded with relief.

By the summer of 1947 I was old enough and strong enough to produce some significant labor and I started working with Grandpa Stowe in his two gardens. He carefully taught me the difference between weeds and vegetables. He couldn't see very well, and I was a great help as I pulled those pesky weeds out of the rows. I soon learned how to use a hoe as he pulled his homemade cultivator between the rows. Every youngster ideally should have a grandfather like George Stowe. He not only taught me how to garden, but there was continuing gentle instruction on work ethic, honesty, fairness, consideration, respect and conscience. He taught by example and pretty much lived by the golden rule.

Grandpa told stories to back up these things too. Let's talk about honesty. He related that at a Sunday get-together for family and friends when he was about twenty, some of the ladies decided it would be nice to have some watermelon. The men took up a collection and came up with one dollar. He and some of the other "young fellas" were dispatched with horse and wagon to a farm near present-day Fourth and Best. The farmer came out to greet them, and they said they had a dollar to spend.

"Fine," he said, "just drive out in that field over yonder and pick up any forty melons you like."

Grandpa's point was, the farmer went back into the house and the boys picked exactly forty melons, didn't do any damage to the property or pick any melons they didn't take. Since the farmer trusted them, it was their obligation to be fair with him—the golden rule in action.

A few off days are bound to happen, and I remember one. I was playing with a neighbor boy, David Hanks, when Grandpa came to get me to do some weeding. I really didn't want to work that day because we were having so much fun, so I asked if

David could come along and help weed, and we would be done in half the time. That seemed to make sense, right?

We didn't weed very long before we started fooling around. I knew we weren't accomplishing much, but I seemed helpless to do anything about it. Before long, Grandpa told us to go on home--that would be enough for the day.

About two hours later he showed up at our place, came in, ran a glass of water, sat down at the kitchen table, took off his hat and waited for the inevitable question.

"How did the weeding go today, Dad?" Mom asked.

Grandpa never bawled me out, but I knew I hadn't done much work, and I stood there with this feeling of doom running up on me.

"Beulah," he said quietly, "you remember that old saying 'Give me one boy and I've got one boy; give me two boys and I have half a boy?' Well, don't worry about it; tomorrow is another day. Larry will do just fine because David will not be coming over again."

That was all there was to it. He hadn't bawled me out or scolded, but I knew what was expected of me and there was never another problem.

One of Grandpa's favorite sayings was, "A job worth doing is worth doing well." An excellent example comes to mind; he decided he wanted to hook up to the sewer. He said very little about it, and I didn't go over to his house for several days. When I did go there was a ditch from the corner of his house to the alley. I can still see it plainly in my mind. He had dug it with a hand shovel and it was unbelievably perfect. The walls were smooth, and I doubt the width varied over one-half inch from end to end or top to bottom. The bottom was perfectly smoothed to the correct pitch, and he was ready to install the pipe. It was a shame to have to fill his masterpiece with dirt.

Coulee Dam had been completed after World War II, and some of our friends had driven over to see it. This had been a major project for our area and this huge dam, located about ninety miles northwest of Spokane, was becoming a popular tourist attraction. One Sunday Dad and Mom decided it was time we made the trip, so we picked up Grandpa Stowe and away we all went. We stopped in a little town in the desert and gassed up the Model A. We hadn't gone very far when we had unwelcome excitement. I was sitting on the left side of the back seat; Ralph was in the middle, with Grandpa on the right. Ralph noticed the right side back door was only halfway latched. He didn't say anything, but decided that it should be closed tightly, and thought he would open it and slam it real quick. This door opened towards the rear of the car (suicide doors, some people called them), and he didn't take into account that we were traveling forty miles an hour. He reached past Grandpa, opened the door, and was sucked out in an instant. Grandpa instinctively grabbed for him as he flashed past, caught him by his right ankle, and held on with all his strength. Dad heard the wind from the open door, slammed on the brakes and stopped. Ralph's hand was still clutching the door handle, Grandpa had his ankle, and even though Ralph was almost entirely out of the car, he had not hit the ground. I give Grandpa full credit for saving Ralph's life. There had been no time to get scared, but now we all were shaking.

We went on to Coulee Dam and did the tourist bit, but it was hard to calm down after this near tragedy.

The excitement wasn't over, though. On the way home that evening we were passing through downtown Spokane. Dad suddenly realized we were coming up on a red light real fast and the car ahead of us had already stopped. He yanked on the emergency brake handle and that locked up the right rear wheel. He swerved hard to the right, cleared the stopped car, and swerved hard to the left. The car rocked violently from side to side as we stopped halfway across the intersection. We had made a terrible screech and had left a very interesting black rubber skid mark on the street. Grandpa cleared his throat rather loudly, but didn't say anything. He was either too scared to speak or couldn't think of anything appropriate to say.

Fifth grade started, and the teacher was none other than the school principal, Gretchen Brautigam. We heard this was her last year, but that didn't mean she was going to relax or turn mellow. She looked as severe as ever, and her long willow switch was displayed prominently in the corner near her desk. Rumor was that she was an expert with it, and that was enough to keep even the ornery kids under control.

Fifth grade class at Harding School, 1947-1948. Custodian, Arta Treman on left, third row and Gretchen Brautigam on right, sitting.

We had a new boy join our Harding School family that year. Bob Cleveland and his parents had moved into 1303 Sherman Avenue. Bob was a tall lanky kid, and he and I hit it off right away. His parents, Larry and Doris, were nice to me, and I began to spend quite a bit of time at their house. Bob came to our place a lot, too. Bob was about a foot taller than I was, and we took some good-natured teasing. Bob's dad sometimes called me "mouse meat," which I hated, but he didn't mean any harm.

For some reason Miss Brautigam took a dislike to Bob, and it was a repeat of the second grade "Dick versus Dewald" situation. Some teachers seem to need a whipping boy. I felt sorry for my new friend as he sat on a stool in the corner and took all sorts of verbal abuse. One day she yelled, "I despise people like you," at him. It was a most upsetting situation for everyone in the class.

Some days Bob had to stay after school for some infraction or other and then, one on one, he told me she did an about-face and was nice to him, helped him with his lessons, and one day offered him a ride home. He thought it best to not break this magic spell and accepted the ride. Then he had to walk back to school to get his bicycle, but decided it was worth the effort if he could get her off his back a little bit.

Bill Gundlach, a newcomer in 4th grade, was also a friend, and I spent a lot of time playing with him, Gene Branson and Duane and David Hanks. My good pal, Jim Abbott, had moved to Sandpoint, but I saw him fairly often when he came to visit his grandparents. I had a detractor here and there, including classmate Donna Pieratt who was considerably taller than I. She started calling me "shrimp salad," and I hated that. If she wanted to get my attention she succeeded, but I scratched her off my list of girls I wanted to marry someday.

One spring day the door to Miss Brautigam's room suddenly opened, and in strode a tall, spare, balding man wearing horn-rimmed glasses. He walked and moved like a man who knew where he was going and what he was about to do. He and Miss Brautigam exchanged pleasantries, and I thought that was pretty neat. She didn't exchange pleasantries very often to my knowledge.

We soon learned that this was Ray Fahringer, the instrumental music instructor for our School District #271. He was on a recruiting visit and invited each of us to start lessons on an instrument next year in 6th grade. He commanded the complete attention of our class as he spoke about the complexities of the various instruments. He came across as a stern fellow, but a man I could get along with. It crossed my mind that maybe I should try playing a violin. It did NOT enter my mind that this man would become a close friend, mentor and guiding light in my life.

After his talk, Miss Brautigam invited him to walk down the hall to see her new building project to add more rooms to our over-crowded school. She asked me to be monitor, to stand at the side blackboard and write down the name of anyone who did not quietly read the assignment she had just made. Talk about a lousy job!

As the two teachers took off down the hall, I peeked out the door and noticed he had his arm around her shoulders as they walked along.

"Yikes," I thought, "who would ever want to hug Miss Brautigam?" I didn't have a clue about the meaning of long-term friendship. None of us had a clue either that her health was failing or that she didn't feel well most days. Maturity has helped me understand her stern and seemingly unreasonable ways. She did retire at the end of that school year and did not live long after that.

I went home from school that day and told Mom about Mr. Fahringer. She remembered him well because he had been teaching music when she went to school. I told her I wanted to learn to play violin. Why? I don't know. She took me seriously and we started looking for a violin to buy. We soon discovered that I was too small to hold a regular violin and we bought a three-quarter size. I started taking lessons from

Mr. Fahringer at the beginning of my sixth grade year.

I am sure that Mom and Dad had hopes that the violin lessons would be more successful than the piano lessons that I took the year before from Sister Theresa, a nun at Immaculate Heart of Mary Academy. We had the beautiful old Stowe family piano in our house and Mom sometimes played it for us after we were in bed. My piano career could only be classed as a study in futility. After a short while Sister Theresa told my parents not to waste any more money. I was hopeless.

The summer between fifth and sixth grades was my time to get my first job. We attended the Church of the Truth at 523 Garden Avenue and when they needed someone to water and mow the lawn, I was hired. I was expected to water the grass two hours every day, unless it was raining, and to mow the grass once a week. The pay was $15 a month. The lawn mower was a hand pusher. I was short, so when the grass got too tall I had a hard time. Then Dad might show up after work and say, "You look a little bit tired. Why don't you rest while I take a few rounds with the mower?" I didn't argue. The hoses also had to be taken out of the church storage room, unrolled, and then rolled up and put away each day after watering. I had a pocket watch and kept a schedule as I moved two sprinklers every ten minutes.

I traveled back and forth from home to church in my Radio Flyer wagon. My right knee rested in the wagon as I pushed with my left leg, steered with my right hand, and held the edge of the wagon bed with my left hand. I don't know why I didn't take the easy way out and just walk.

At the end of the summer I had $45 and my parents took me shopping for my first bicycle. We found a real nice Columbia bike for $38 at the Lighthouse Sporting Goods Store, 305 Sherman, and made the deal. I was thrilled-- this was one of the happiest days of my life. As time went on I added mud flaps with reflectors on them, a basket, rear view mirror, hand-squeezed horn and a coon tail. I didn't have a Schwinn like some boys had, but my Columbia was accessorized nicely.

In 1949 sixth grade got underway with a new school principal and sixth grade teacher. Duane Harrison was a veteran of World War II and had married an English lady while overseas. He had a ready smile, was well organized, and wanted everything to be nice and orderly as he taught. When some of the boys misbehaved, he lost his temper and they found out he could be as tough as he needed to be. As a last resort he would take the problem lad out into the hall, request him to bend over and hold his ankles. The large, heavy paddle went SMACK! If the kid smiled or laughed he got another one. Repeat offenders didn't exist.

One day each week at 8 a.m., we instrumental types walked to the Junior High School at Seventh and Montana for a class lesson with Mr. Fahringer. He had a large room in the basement of the school and we sat on chairs around the edges. Bob Boughton, Jean Ross and Jean Olson started on clarinet. Gene Branson and Bill Gundlach took trumpet. Students from Bryan and Central schools were there at the same time. We each got our turn to play our instrument as Mr. Fahringer moved from student to student. We were expected to be quiet and learn from the other students' attempts. If we talked, we got a sharp look and a loud snap of his fingers. Nobody got much playing time, but we learned to play in front of an audience. He was a stern, no-nonsense teacher, and if he thought you were trying and practicing, he was gentle, quiet and very helpful. Obviously he knew exactly what he was talking about. Lazy or smart aleck kids were given two or three chances to mend their ways and, if they didn't, were invited to not come back. Those students were referred to as "deadwood," and they were "trimmed out."

Mr. Fahringer was in control of his room one hundred percent of the time and made the most of the limited time he had with his students each week. Discipline was number one, music was number two. It was exactly what every child needed and most didn't get.

The sixth graders were the "big kids" so we got to take turns being crossing guards at 15th and Sherman. The traffic volume was light by today's standards, but nevertheless, Sherman Avenue was still U.S. Highway 10, the forerunner of Interstate 90. All the freight and logging trucks traveled this street and there was no traffic light. We had to wear a white, three-inch-wide strap that crisscrossed our upper body, and we had a short handled wooden stop sign about twelve inches across.

We were there to help younger students cross a dangerous street, but now I wonder how drivers even noticed us. I remember how important and powerful I felt when it was "necessary" to stop a big freight truck; pretty heady stuff for an eleven- or twelve-year-old. Miraculously, I don't remember anybody ever getting hurt.

Now that I had a bicycle a whole new world opened up. Bob Cleveland, Gene Branson and Bill Gundlach were my main riding partners and we went all over the area. Nobody worried about us if we rode around Fernan Lake, along the highway around Coeur d'Alene Lake, out to Dalton Gardens, or to the Spokane River. We often picked up beer and pop bottles as we rode, which we sold at various grocery stores. Beer bottles fetched a penny and pop bottles were good for three cents. That gave us money to buy pop and candy that our parents didn't know about.

It was our 6th grade winter when Bob and I decided we wanted to become ice fishermen. We saw people fishing on the ice at Fernan Lake and thought it appeared to be an enjoyable way to spend a winter afternoon.

We collected all the gear we thought we needed, and Bob's Dad agreed to drive us out to the first wide spot on Fernan Lake Road. He helped us unload, smiled broadly and cheerily told us to have a good time.

"I'll be back in three hours," he said as he hopped into his toasty warm car and waved goodbye.

We were excited about our adventure as we carried our fishing gear to a likely looking place on the ice. We returned to the road and each rolled an old tire onto the ice to burn to keep ourselves warm in the 20-degree weather. This was traditional in those days and the bottom of the lake is no doubt littered with thousands of miles of wire from those tires.

First we had to chop a hole in the ice. I started chopping and Bob said he would build the fire. I didn't know how resistant ice was; fine particles of ice sprayed my face and coat as I chopped with the hatchet. I didn't know ice could be so cold!

Bob, meanwhile, discovered that kindling and newspaper wouldn't necessarily quickly ignite a tire. After about an hour we had a hole broken through about eight or ten inches of ice, were both covered with ice particles, and had a fire that produced thick black choking smoke that chased us wherever we stood; nobody had mentioned how stinky tire smoke was either. The breeze seemed to blow the heat from the fire away from us as it blew the smoke towards us, and we realized we should have worn several more coats and pairs of pants because standing on ice is COLD. Since it is impossible to bait a hook with corn or fish eggs while wearing gloves, our hands soon felt like chunks of ice and then the corn and fish eggs froze solid. I didn't even care that I caught a seven-inch perch. Bob's watch indicated we still had one hour and forty-three minutes until his dad would pick us up. That was a long time to have "fun" as we stomped our feet and ran around in circles trying to keep warm.

When Larry Cleveland came to get us he was right on time. Bob and I were almost as stiff as the four little perch we had caught.

"I could have told you all the reasons I gave up ice fishing thirty years ago," he said cheerfully, "but you wouldn't have believed me."

Things were improving at our house. Aunt Alma shipped us her old refrigerator on the train when she bought a new one, and we finally got a telephone—our number was 356J2—and it was a four-party line. This was exciting as I learned how to place a call. Lift the receiver, wait, and hopefully, before too long, a woman's voice said, "Number, please."

After receiving the number the operator said, "Thank you." Each phone call required a short visit with the operator and, if she was acquainted with the caller, she might even repeat a little tidbit of local gossip. In those days the operator was always a woman.

Dad was busy improving our house. By now we had wall switches to turn on most of our lights and he added several outlets. He bought a book and learned how to do it himself. He bought salvaged insulation from Farragut, insulated our attic and stuffed it down the walls where he could reach. He crawled under the house and with the aid of some jacks, installed supports to level our floors and then laid new linoleum. He hired a neighbor, Ed Poehler, to help, and they built a concrete block foundation under the back wall that had been sitting on rotting timbers. He also built cabinets to replace the shelves in the kitchen. Now that Dad had a full-time, secure job, our household was much more stable and we lived a lot better.

Somewhere along the way Dad had acquired an axle with wheels attached, and he proceeded to use this to build a new trailer. This made a lot of sense because our Model A Ford did not have a trunk, and there was really no way to haul much of anything in or on the car. He built a well-thought-out trailer with a box about eight feet in length. There was a tailgate that opened on hinges, and the front of the box was a board that slid out easily in case he wanted to haul long boards. The tongue (the board between the trailer box and the hitch) was about five feet long, and he used a nice red fir 2x10 plank for this.

There was no city garbage collection so we needed to go to the city dump from time to time. This was always an interesting way to spend a Sunday afternoon. Dad would get the trailer loaded, and then ask, "Anybody want to make a quick trip to the dump?"

There often wasn't much action around the neighborhood on Sunday, so why not?

We would journey north on 15th Street to Best Avenue and turn west. As is the case today, Best Avenue abruptly became Appleway Avenue at 4th Street. Why? Because the town grew in segments, let's call them little islands in the woods. As these segments grew together, some strange things sometimes happened.

In this case Best Avenue existed from 4th to 15th with the Best family scattered along its length. At about 8th Street several Best families built houses, and in 1893 established their own family cemetery, located about two blocks north of Best Avenue. Hope Cemetery still exists, has been donated to the nonprofit Share Hope Memorial Gardens, and restoration is ongoing.

Appleway was the main highway entering Coeur d'Alene from Spokane, and before it terminated at 4th Street, the road made a long curve southward and joined 4th Street about two hundred feet south of where Best joined 4th. As time went on, people started cutting across the field from Best to Appleway to avoid the jog and the big curve, and sometime in the 1930s this shortcut became a street. The triangular area in the middle was large enough for the North Star Service Station and a house that remained there until the sixties. So Appleway and Best were hooked up, but each street retained its own name.

As we traveled between 4th Street and Government Way, we always admired the Perl Bailey farm on the north side of Appleway. The farm's focal point was a big windmill about where Hastings Music Store is now located. This neighborhood was sparsely populated with a few service stations, restaurants, motels and taverns, mixed in with farmhouses and a chicken ranch. Government Way was still U.S. 95, and the intersection with Appleway was considered busy and dangerous. The whole area was "out in the country."

The turnoff to the dump was about where Julia Street now intersects Appleway. About one-quarter mile to the north we drove down a long hill into what seemed to be a vast network of narrow roads winding around huge piles of garbage, stumps and junk of every kind. There was usually a pall of smoke over the general vicinity because part of the dump was always on fire or at least smoldering.

The scary part, however, were the gunshots. The Sunday afternoon sport for many gun enthusiasts was to shoot rats at the dump. When a bullet would go zinging off a rock or some hard object Mom got real jumpy, and Ralph and I had to stay in the car. I don't know why--the old Model A sure wasn't bullet-proof.

The real adventure started after Dad spotted a likely looking place to unload and started to back up. The trailer seemed to develop a mind of its own, and all too often it would jackknife; if Dad didn't stop immediately, there would be a loud "KEEE-RAKK," and his nice red fir tongue would shatter into kindling wood. Trailer backing was not his best area of expertise.

After he unloaded he would have to lash the trailer to our car bumper with the tow chain and hope it held. Before we could go home it was customary to look around and check out what other people had dumped, just in case there were some items we could use. There was usually something "perfectly good" to be loaded into our trailer.

Mom didn't much care for this smoky, stinky, swap meet unless we drove by a pile where somebody had dumped the contents of a house that had been cleaned out after a death. These were the days before yard and garage sales; sometimes people got in a hurry and took pots and pans, dishes, vases, fruit jars, etc. to the dump. When this happened Mom leaped out of the car to glean for possible treasures, forgetting all about the gunshots and men shouting, "Hey, I got a big one!"

Of course, there was an endless supply of nails, screws, and broken glass to run over, so it wasn't too unusual to have a flat tire before we got back to Appleway Avenue. If it was a rear tire, there was the added challenge of getting the car jacked up with a trailer lashed to its bumper.

Sometimes it was dark before we got home and we were tired and hungry. In retrospect—instead of a quick trip it had actually been an adventuresome ordeal that took hours. The fire would have gone out in the cook stove and dinner would be late.

A trip to the dump these days just isn't any kind of an adventure at all. Dad would be appalled—unloading inside a building with an attendant to guide you, after driving across a scale to weigh the whole outfit. It's so bad that there is a rule forbidding the sport of checking out other people's throwaways.

Dad's trailer was the source of other wildly entertaining escapades. One Sunday he and Mom went to visit friends at their ranch near Squaw Bay on Coeur d'Alene Lake. Fortunately I had something else to do that day. Part of the plan was to take the trailer so that they could bring home a big load of cow manure to spread on our garden. After their visit they were rolling along toward home with a full load, mission accomplished. They drove around the curve where Beauty Bay joins Wolf Lodge Bay and the left trailer wheel fell off. It rolled across the highway, down the embankment and into the lake. This resulted in an abrupt stop for the up-to-then happy travelers.

The wheel was floating in the lake, but Dad couldn't begin to reach it, so he walked more than a mile to a house near the east end of Wolf Lodge Bay and borrowed a rowboat. He rowed along the embankment, retrieved his wheel and got it to shore. Then he had to row the boat home and walk back to the car. He had a terrible time getting the trailer jacked up to put the wheel on, and when he did he had another problem. The lug nuts had come off because he had forgotten to tighten them completely after changing a flat tire. They were gone forever, so he removed one nut from each of the car wheels, and they made it home without further mishap. Dad rarely gave up and admitted defeat.

In the spring of my 6th grade school year Dr. Fred Horning informed Mom and Dad that my tonsils were causing me a lot of trouble, and they had to go. Dr. Horning had his office at 421 Coeur d'Alene Avenue and he did minor surgeries in the basement of this building.

So one sunny morning it was time for my introduction to ether. This was a rather cruel way to put a little kid to sleep, and I didn't like it one bit as I tried to hold my breath. When I finally had to take a deep breath it was all over.

I got to go home in late afternoon. I felt terrible and got sick in the back seat of our car. That was par for the course for that poor old back seat.

Bob Cleveland came to see me that evening. He said "hello," took one look at me, spun around and ran out the front door. He told me later that I looked so sick and was so white he thought I was going to die for sure. He ran out because he didn't want to be on the premises when I passed over. I fooled him, ate lots of ice cream, chewed Aspergum and got well. My general health was immediately better, and I began to

Doris Gammel with daughters, Janis and MaryLynn, in 1948. Photo courtesy of MaryLynn Gammel Strickland.

grow and gain weight.

June of 1949 started with a trip to Kirby, Wyoming to visit Uncle John and Aunt Doris, MaryLynn and Janis. This was their new home after the sale of the Glendive, Montana tire shop. Mom had been reluctant to go, but Dad had some work done on the Ford and was very convincing when he said the car was in great shape.

Two weeks before we were to leave Dad turned into our driveway and the right rear wheel fell off; it rolled almost to 16th Street. Mom laughed hysterically about that little episode, but Dad convinced her the car axle was safely repaired, and we left for Wyoming pulling the trailer loaded with our suitcases and a rollaway bed. Aunt Doris was short of beds so we just took our own. Not everybody takes a bed along when they go visiting, but this seemed normal to me.

We journeyed along pretty well until we arrived at Yellowstone Park and ran into a blizzard. We drove past a horrific head-on wreck. A little farther on the Ford coughed and stopped and Dad got out with an old rag to see if the problem was wet wires. I am still amazed that he dried wires somewhere and the car started. Oh, for the simplicity of a Model A Ford!

We made it over the pass and eased through Buffalo Bill Canyon; it was a super scary road featuring sheer rock cliffs and steep embankments down to the river. We stayed in Cody, Wyoming that night in a brand-new log motel.

The next day we arrived at Gammels'. Their house was long and narrow and almost everyone slept in the one main room except Dad and Mom. They slept in the kitchen where the refrigerator motor was so loud they complained they couldn't sleep much.

We kids discovered gumbo mud the next day when we went out to play. The farther we walked the taller we got, but pretty soon our feet were so heavy we couldn't move. Then we took a ride, got into the gumbo mud, and pretty soon the wheels wouldn't turn anymore and we were stuck. I guess we had a good time, but I was not very impressed with Wyoming.

Aunt Doris decided to bring the two girls and travel back to Coeur d'Alene with us to visit for a week or two. This was interesting with seven people in a Model A. Those cars were narrow inside because the running boards took up so much room. It seemed like every five minutes or so somebody needed a drink or a bathroom stop or something. It was hot and miserable in the car. Aunt Doris drove part of the time, and she liked to cut across the curves if no car was coming toward us. Dad was jumpy about this, but she said it was okay because it cut down the mileage, saved gas, and we would get home quicker. She had an answer for everything.

If it had been ten or fifteen years earlier we would have been mistaken for a family fleeing Oklahoma. When we stopped at a motel for the night Dad made a deal with the motel owner, and we got a better rate because we had a bed we could unload and set up in our room. See? That proves it makes sense to take a bed along when you go on vacation.

The next day was still hot and sweaty, and MaryLynn was complaining about not feeling well. About mid-morning it became obvious that she was breaking out with three-day measles. That wasn't bad enough; the car started backfiring and then stopped. We were near a little town, and a mechanic came, tinkered around for a while and the car started right up.

"Well, that wasn't too bad," said Dad.

"Don't kid yourself, Earl," said Aunt Doris, "we aren't going very far because the coil is going bad."

He didn't think she knew anything about cars and ignored the remark.

A few minutes later we were stopped again.

A car stopped to help and one of the men in it was a mechanic. He found a connection in the wiring where there were two washers installed instead of one, and said that was causing a short. Sure enough, the car started right up.

"We better stop in Missoula and buy a coil," advised Aunt Doris. "Every time we stop it cools off and then the car will start again. When it gets hot it is no good. That is how a worn-out coil often acts."

Dad was getting rather annoyed with his sister-in-law at this point and said, "That mechanic found the trouble, and we are doing just fine. We've got a sick girl and I'm going to keep going."

Seven miles west of Missoula there was one big backfire and the motor stopped.

After several "I told you so's," from Aunt Doris, Dad gave up and glumly said, "Well, there is only one thing to do. I will hitch-hike back to Missoula and buy a coil."

It was a hot, miserable two hours of waiting while cars roared past us and rocked our car back and forth. He finally made it back with a new coil, installed it, and the motor started right up.

Summer of 1949, left to right, Janis Gammel in basket, Larry Strobel, Doris Gammel, MaryLynn Gammel and Ralph Strobel. Photo courtesy of MaryLynn Gammel Strickland.

We made it home sometime after dark and Aunt Doris was very proud of her auto diagnostic ability. All our friends and relatives heard that story, but Dad never told it.

Seventh grade was at the Junior High School at 7th and Montana. We had a homeroom and then went to five additional rooms during the day. The music kids were all in room 7-1 and stayed together all day as we moved through the different classes. Bertha Meyer was our homeroom teacher.

Miss Meyer was a tall, spare, spinster lady and we unkindly called her "Beanpole Bertha" behind her back. She was rather eccentric and seemed to be a nervous wreck as she fought for some semblance of control in the classroom. Some days she was so over-wrought she was reduced to tears, and I still feel guilty because we weren't very nice to her. She meant well and was trying to hang on to qualify for retirement. We were no help.

My violin playing was slowly improving and though quite a few of the students who started had already quit, I stayed with it. The band and orchestra kids stuck together and were most of my best friends. Twelve of us from Harding School had already gone to school together for six years. People didn't move around nearly so much in those days.

Even at this point Ray Fahringer was a positive influence in my life. I was basically afraid of him, yet realized he liked me and was trying to be helpful. I admired the way he handled disruptive students, especially non-music students who crossed him. One day during a class lesson there was quite a commotion in the hall. Mr. Fahringer stepped out to see what was going on and told the troublemaker to quiet down.

"You aren't my teacher, you can't tell me what to do," sneered the boy.

Oh, what a mistake that was!

This man of sixty-one years picked Mr. Loudmouth up by the front of his shirt, slammed him against the lockers and held him there with his feet six inches off the floor.

"Boy," he thundered, "Don't you ever speak to me like that again!"

Some people may not have liked Ray Fahringer, but respect was a requirement.

Coeur d'Alene High School Band and Orchestra concerts were big events during these years, and some concerts were repeated to accommodate overflow crowds at the beautiful high school auditorium located on the 3rd floor. The band and orchestra also rehearsed on the stage in this auditorium daily—orchestra Tuesday and Thursday and band Monday, Wednesday and Friday.

There were few people in town who didn't know Ray Fahringer. He played golf, tennis and went hunting with some of the biggest names in Coeur d'Alene. Bankers, doctors, lawyers and lumbermen were his friends. When he needed musical equipment and the school district had no money for it, he was known to make bets on the golf course and usually won—providing money for the new equipment.

For all his seeming confidence he had seen his share of troubled times. He married his first wife, Olive, in 1910, but her health was poor and they had no children. She was stricken with multiple sclerosis and was confined to a wheelchair for several years before dying in 1917 at age twenty-nine.

Ray had come to Coeur d'Alene in 1915 to take over the instrumental music program for School District 271. In 1918 he went into the Navy and played trombone in a Navy band until the war ended. He returned to Coeur d'Alene after the war and in 1920 married Veronica "Vera" Day. Their son, Raymond James, Jr. (Jimmie), was born in 1923. Their lives were shattered when Jimmie died in 1926 from a viral infection. In 1931 they adopted Bob and, as luck would have it, this boy had perfect pitch and he learned to play excellent violin and clarinet.

The winter of 1949-1950 was one of the coldest, snowiest and longest ever recorded in North Idaho. Coeur d'Alene Lake was frozen over by December 15th, 1949. Grandpa Stowe had never seen it freeze before January in his sixty-one years as a Coeur d'Alene resident. The snow kept piling up and the temperature kept going down. The three-foot fence between our house and the next-door neighbor disappeared. In one ten-day period the highest temperature recorded was 16 degrees, and the low bottomed out at -30 degrees. In mid-January schools closed for over two weeks because it was impossible to keep the buildings heated, and cars that would start became scarce.

Friday, January 13th, 1950 is a date that is very memorable. A fierce blizzard was underway by 1 pm and school was soon dismissed. My mile walk home was extremely cold with the snow whipped by a lively northwest wind. The temperature was about 5 degrees and who knows what the wind chill factor was. It hadn't been invented yet.

School District 271 had only three school buses and before long they were stuck in snowdrifts as they tried to get the students home. Wreckers pulled the buses free, they went back to town, and those kids ended up staying at motels for the night. Cars were buried in snowdrifts all over the Rathdrum Prairie and Hayden Lake area. The Highway 10 underpass just west of Post Falls was the scene of a wreck and, before it could be cleared away, the underpass filled with snow and the highway was closed. Many Coeur d'Alene residents worked at Kaiser Aluminum in the Spokane valley as my Dad did. None of these people got home that night. Dad was holed up in the Stone Church at McGuire with a lot of other Kaiser employees. Many were stranded at the State Line Village in one of the taverns or nightclubs there. Slot machines were still legal, and stories were widespread about men who blew their weekly paycheck before the blizzard stopped.

When I got home from school before 3 pm I shoveled a trail to our woodshed and brought in a good supply. It went fast in the bitter cold and when I decided to go for more wood at 7 pm there was no sign of where my trail had been.

The storm let up about midnight, and Dad finally got home about 5 a.m. I have seen very few storms since to equal that one. Just about everyone had a story to tell.

Coeur d'Alene Lake froze deeper and deeper as the January and early February temperatures were dropping from 0 to –30 every night. Some people drove their cars and trucks on the frozen lake clear to Harrison; the ice was plenty thick, but snowdrifts were a problem. We had snow on the ground until the end of March, and the lake wasn't ice-free until early April.

The summer of 1950 was a busy time. I still took care of the lawn at the church. I had five lawns to mow and I worked as a cherry picker in Grandpa Stowe's old orchard. The pay for this hot, sticky job was 5 cents for each pound picked. Uncle Jasper and Aunt Ruth owned the property now, and my cousins George, Phyllis, Donna and

Walter Hogeweide were the main pickers. George was the champion picker; it looked to me that all he had to do was set his ladder up by the tree, climb up, wave his arms around a few times, and he would climb down with a bucketful. He taught me well, and I became a proficient picker.

One summer Phyllis, unknown to George, decided to dethrone him as the champion picker. She planned carefully; she knew she could pick while he was making two trips a day to the Cannery in Post Falls. She quietly and methodically worked at top speed and at the end of the season had picked more than one thousand pounds of cherries. She won!

Sometimes I rode with George when he took a load of cherries to Seiters' Cannery on the western edge of Post Falls, which is ten miles west of Coeur d'Alene. This very large wooden building was a landmark for many years. They hired dozens of local people to process the fruits and vegetables grown on hundreds of small farms in north Idaho and the Spokane valley.

Many farmers also kept a herd of dairy cows. The Coeur d'Alene Creamery was at First and Garden; every morning there was a steady stream of trucks and pickups arriving to unload metal milk cans onto the Creamery loading dock. This thriving business bottled milk and cream, made ice cream, butter and cottage cheese. It was located north of the Roosevelt School and covered half a city block.

There were still a number of dairies around that bottled their own milk and cream every day. After it was bottled, one of the family members drove a milk route and delivered milk and cream to customers. These routes overlapped and competition was fierce at times. We usually bought milk from Frank Whitesitt who had a dairy at Meadowbrook. If we had unexpected company and needed extra milk, we would watch for Alice Carnie from Mica Flats to go by, flag her down, and buy more milk from her.

This was the summer of "the bike wreck." I was in a hurry to get home from downtown one afternoon and was really whizzing along—eastbound on Sherman Avenue. It is a bit downhill between 11th and 12th Streets and I picked up more speed. In front of Redmond's Grocery Store at 1200 Sherman I saw a flash of blue and "CRASH!" A woman with a brand new two-door Buick convertible had swung her door open without looking in her mirror. What happened next would have been a credit to a Hollywood stunt man. I rode my bike through a complete somersault over that door and landed on the wheels. I bounced once and fell over on my left side. I was afraid a car would run over me from behind and scrambled to get out of the street. I didn't need to worry—I noticed the cars behind me had all stopped. The wire basket on the front of my bike was about the thickness of a pancake, the fork was sprung, the chain was off the sprocket, and one of the permanently glued-on handle grips that could never be removed was lying in the street. I knew they had been permanently glued because the neighbor kids and I had tried all summer to pull them off.

I had small scrapes on my left knee and left elbow, and a nick on my left ear. The lady driver was frantically checking me over, holding my hand and calling me "dear" and "honey." I was in a bit of shock, but I think she was worse off than I was. I put the chain back on and rode slowly home.

Dad tried to straighten out the basket, but it was never the same. He was skeptical of my story, but our neighbors, Victor and Loreta Cook, had been right behind me and confirmed what I said. It slowly dawned on me how lucky I was to be alive. Interestingly enough, my glasses hadn't even flown off.

Later that summer Dad was late getting home from work one night and when he drove into our driveway he wasn't in the Model A Ford. Instead he parked a black 1938 Plymouth sedan, and tried to nonchalantly stroll into the house.

"Whose car is that?" queried Mom.

"Ours!" he answered. "The old Ford was really worn out—it was time to get something newer."

He knew that Mom would have a "hissy fit" if he mentioned trading cars. He had to tell her sooner or later, and he had opted for later. It was a done deal.

"I didn't even get to tell the old car goodbye," she sobbed as she burst into tears.

I thought it was great. Gone were "the pit" backseat and the leaky roof. This car even had a trunk, wider tires and more room inside. At only twelve years old it seemed practically new. Dad had made a good move, and I was old enough to know that Mom would get acquainted with the new car before too long.

The 8th grade was a good year for me. My homeroom teacher was Helen McQuaig, a teacher of great ability; a pleasant, warm, smiling lady who obviously loved what she was doing and she was good at it.

My violin playing was getting better and I had moved up from poor to fair to mediocre. I was not yet an inspired music student and I wanted to quit. Mom wouldn't hear of it, and I kept plugging along. Some days when I was splitting wood and kindling, I would consider cutting the end off my left hand little finger so that I could quit, but I wasn't that brave and repeatedly abandoned the idea. I was a "dumbkid" (that is all one word), but not that dumb.

Downtown Coeur d'Alene was a beehive of activity. Virtually every doctor, dentist and lawyer had his or her office downtown. JC Penney's at 317 Sherman (now Brix Restaurant), Montgomery Ward's at 119 North 4th (later Wiggett's Antique Mall) and Woolworth's, 314 Sherman were the "big stores." Menswear was found at Gridley's Men's Store, 223 Sherman and IXL Toggery, 311 Sherman. Ladies' fine clothing was sold at Grace Hall Apparel, 200 4th, The Fashionette, 217 Sherman and The Coeur d'Alene Style Shop, where Grace Anderson specialized in "foundations." The Oda May Shop, 222 Sherman, was a tiny shop with beautiful jewelry, handkerchiefs and gifts. Ben Franklin, 301 Sherman, Hart Drug Store, 324 Sherman, Wilson's Drug at 401 Sherman, Dingle's Hardware, 402 Sherman, Burch Furniture, 408 Sherman, Gardner's Auto Supply at 501 Sherman, Everson's Jewelry, 109 N. 4th, Overjorde's Jewelry, 309 Sherman and Evergreen Floral, 213 Sherman were all busy, successful businesses in the 1940s and 1950s.

The floors in Montgomery Ward's always made loud, unique, squeaking sounds. Some things don't change and that floor still sounds just the same. At Penney's none of the clerks ever ran a cash register. A receipt was written and it, along with money handed over, was inserted into a can-type holder with a screw top, which was attached to a cable. Pull the handle attached to the cable and the can went zipping up to the lady cashier situated on the balcony. The customer's change and receipt in the can soon came sliding down the cable; the clerk opened the can and gave them to the customer.

Nobody seemed to mind waiting as clerk and customer visited. The merchandise was usually wrapped in brown paper and tied with string.

If car shopping was the business of the day it was definitely done downtown. The choices were many—E.R. Elliott Ford 502 Sherman, Knudtsen Chevrolet at 301 North 4th, Kramer Pontiac, 416 Coeur d'Alene Avenue, Freeland-Wyman Dodge-Plymouth at 400 North 4th, Koenig Kennedy Buick, 309 Lakeside Avenue, Broderick Motors Oldsmobile and Cadillac at 204 North 2nd, Pool Motors-Studebaker, 118 North 2nd and Central Motors at 212 Sherman to buy a Hudson car or International truck. All had showrooms and lots that we thought contained an ample variety of vehicles. By today's standards these agencies were miniscule.

Lake City General Hospital was at 412 Lakeside Avenue. Ironically, it sat next to the Elks Lodge, which was three times the size of the hospital. The Eagles Lodge was and is at 209 Sherman. The "big" grocery store was Safeway at 308 Lakeside Avenue. That entire store would have been approximately equal to the produce department and four or five aisles of today's Albertson's. Other downtown groceries were Independent Market 204 N. 4th, Metropole 310 Sherman, A & H Market 412 Sherman and Clodius' Grocery 415 Sherman.

There were at least fifteen downtown taverns, and the better known places like the Club Cigar 313 Sherman, Fritz's Corner 302 Sherman, and Seymour's Cigar 202 Sherman had poker games in their back rooms. This was still legal in 1950 as were slot machines. Some men made their living playing poker—they went to "work" every day. It was almost impossible for an "outsider" to beat up on a "regular" as the two or three regulars at a table would gang up on the innocent tourist, lumberjack

Templin's Bar and Grill, ca. 1950, 112 Sherman Avenue. Museum of North Idaho photo.

fresh from the woods, or a mill worker looking for a little payday fun.

Downtown restaurants included The Brunswick at 411 Sherman (it had slot machines), Fowler's, 122 N. 4th, Sugar Bowl, 308 Sherman, Silver Grill, 304 Sherman, Club Café (later Merrill's) at 313 ½ Sherman, Missouri Lunch (later Hudson's Hamburgers), 210 Sherman and Templin's Bar and Grill at 112 West Sherman.

If we wanted an ice cream treat we had our choice of Woolworth's lunch counter, Wilson's Drugstore Fountain or The D'Alene Ice Cream Shop at 319 Coeur d'Alene Avenue—the best of all, owned by Clarence and Noleen Buch. They made their own ice cream and had fancy metal tables and chairs. Their little boy rode his tricycle around in the shop and visited with the customers. Vicki Faulkner Johnson recalls working there in 1944, scooping ice cream for 10 cents an hour.

While it was true that the bulk of the business was transacted downtown there was a convenience called "The Neighborhood Grocer" who seemed to be located in every neighborhood. It was rare if a store wasn't within easy walking distance of most homes. Many of these grocery stores were located in the former living room of a house with the grocer and his family living upstairs, in the back or in the basement. Typically, shopping took a while. The customer came into the store with a list and waited while the proprietor walked around collecting the desired items, which were piled on the counter. While this was being done a steady exchange of gossip and information was exchanged. This slow-paced, low-stress lifestyle somehow has been replaced by labor-saving, cost-cutting, time-saving devices invented to supposedly make our lives more efficient.

Some of these Mom and Pop stores I remember were the Wayside Grocery at 1613 Sherman Avenue operated by Karl and Dora Arneson, grandparents of my good friend, Jim Abbott. Entry was by way of a wooden bridge and we shopped there several times a week. A popular, busy Hedal's Grocery, located at 2215 Sherman Avenue had a glass-topped gas pump out front. Tall Pine Grocery at 305 South 15th Street, Hultman's Grocery at 509 North 15th Street, Mac's Grocery at 212 North 13th, Home Grocery at 322 South 11th Street, 10th St. Grocery at 207 North 10th Street, Eggart's Grocery at 718 North 10th Street, Driessen's Grocery at 824 Wallace Avenue and Jordan's Grocery at 1036 North 15th with a beauty shop in back were all in the east end of town. Two "big" stores were McEuen's 12th Street IGA at 1123 Sherman and Redmond's East End Grocery at 1200 Sherman.

It was stores galore on 7th Street with Withers' (later Whitely's) at 310 North 7th and Smith's Grocery at 516 North 7th. Across from the High School, The Viking was at 811 North 7th, The White Pine at 815 North 7th and Stark's (later Mark's) Table Supply at 825 North 7th. Made for a busy block, Stark's was a bigger store with six apartments upstairs. The 7th Street Grocery (later Withers') at 919 North 7th, Troutman's Grocery at 625 East Harrison and Merkel's Grocery at 703 East Harrison all stayed busy. Merkel's had the advantage of two gas pumps out front.

Moving west across town, Fields' Grocery was at 1401 North 4th. Kamp Komfort Kabin Kamp at 1710 North 4th was a combination store, gas station with glass-topped pumps, upstairs apartments and cabins out back. Camp Joy at 1902 North 4th was similar. Iverson's Grocery was at 418 Reid with Hilgren's Grocery at 1201 Government Way enjoying the advantage of gas pumps. This one later became Gittel's. Lincoln

Jim Abbott and his grandfather, Karl Arneson, owner of Wayside Grocery, 1613 Sherman Avenue. The store was in the original living room. Photo courtesy of Jim Abbott.

Way Food Shop was at 1604 Lincoln Way. Two bigger stores were Payless Grocery at 811 North 4th and Long's Food Market at 818 North 4th.

Pearl Baker had a store at 903 B Street and Dutch and Mary Ott ran Dutch's Grocery at 128 Wallace Avenue. Two stores in the Fort Grounds were the Confectionery at 705 River Avenue and the Acton brothers' "big" Fort Grounds Grocery and Market at 810 River Avenue. Oliver ran a well-stocked meat market in the back of the store and Merle ran the grocery part. A large apartment was upstairs.

Closer to downtown were Park Drive Grocery at 245 Northwest Boulevard and Lakeview Court Grocery at 264 Northwest Boulevard, operated by Al Gittel. Lakeview Court next door, owned by Wes Hamlet, covered about three acres and featured beautiful lawns and huge pine trees with 24 little white cabins scattered throughout the property. They were a popular destination for tourists who returned there each summer—right across from the City Beach and Park. Their sprinkling system was unique—at least three Little Black Sambo sprinklers. These were brightly-colored wooden cut-outs of a black boy about four feet tall hooked to a garden hose and held upright by a spike that was pushed into the lawn. The water pressure caused the sprinkler to move back and forth in a wide arc with the appearance that little Sambo was holding a sprinkling nozzle in his right hand. They were a novelty and a popular tourist attraction in those years.

Customary closing time for stores was 6 pm Monday through Saturday and they were closed on Sunday. If a person really needed an item when the store was closed you could knock at the back door and, if someone was home, you would be let in

Lakeview Court Cabins and Grocery. Museum of North Idaho photo.

and could make your purchase. These were family stores and most were friendly and accommodating.

Some of the store owners allowed "credit" to their trusted customers. A box of notepads was kept under the counter with each customer's name written on the end. When "Mrs. Jones" came in, her purchases were handwritten with the price noted on the right side of the pad. It was customary to settle up at the first of the month. Sometimes men were out of work and couldn't pay for several months and then would spend half the summer trying to catch up. Most people paid up eventually. The grocer was a friend and it was not acceptable to beat him out of his money.

I visited most of these stores over the years. My brother, Ralph, started a bottle cap collection the summer before I entered 8th grade. It started as a nice little collection to display a cap from every type and brand of pop available in our area. All pop was marketed in glass bottles with a variety of shapes and sizes—most of them painted with the name of the pop and bottling company. Some I remember were Pepsi-Cola, Coca-Cola, Dr. Pepper, Nu Grape, Orange Crush, 7 UP, Bubble Up, Dad's Root Beer, B-1 Lemon Lime, Nesbitt Orange, Canada Dry Ginger Ale, Squirt, Orange Kist, Nehi Grape and other flavors and Mason's Old-fashioned Root Beer.

A local bottler was Ralph's Beverage Company, located at 902 Lincoln Way, owned by Ralph Anderson. His bottles were easily recognized by the tall, skinny ornate shape. "Ralph's Beverages" was painted on the bottle and the bottle cap identified the flavor. Coca-Cola Bottling was at 1424 Sherman and Pepsi-Cola Bottling was at 1602 Sherman. If we were out riding our bikes in the evening and stopped to peer in the window to watch the bottles go around the conveyor, an employee might motion for us to go around to the back door. He would invite us in to watch the bottling process and give us each a bottle of pop. Rules were casual.

Every store had a large water-filled cooler. The water was kept cold by an electrified refrigeration unit. On the side of the cooler there was an attached bottle opener with a hook-on metal container to catch the caps so they wouldn't fall on the floor.

My brother started asking the various store owners if he could empty their bottle cap containers as he looked for new and unusual caps. The problem was he kept them all, and after several neighbor boys and I decided to help him the collection grew rapidly. Before long there were boxes of bottle caps sitting on the back porch, in the yard and garage and Dad's supply of wooden boxes was depleted. Sometimes a little pop spilled as the cap was removed so the container was full of sticky caps. A box of sticky bottle caps sitting in the summer sun created a rather unpleasant odor, and before long Dad decided this bottle-cap business was completely out of control. He had been patient as Ralph sorted the day's "take" every evening, but I could tell he was becoming annoyed. I heard him talking to Mom about a way to get rid of this expanding problem without hurting Ralph's feelings.

Dad was doing more remodeling and had built the forms for a new concrete front porch to replace the rotting wooden one.

"You can really help me," he told Ralph. "It is going to take an awful lot of expensive concrete to build the new porch and I need something to use as fill when I pour the concrete. Why don't you keep one of each kind of cap and I will use the rest to fill in as I pour the concrete."

Strobel family with cat, Sam, in front of new front porch.

Ralph was reluctant at first, but decided to go along with the plan and dumped box after box of caps as he helped the family save some money.

If anybody ever jackhammers that porch he will get a surprise, and forever wonder why there are thousands of bottle caps buried in the concrete.

In the early spring of 1949 the Giovenelli family moved in across the street at 1504 Coeur d'Alene Avenue. The gossipy neighbor ladies were soon discussing the "Italian family from back east." They eyed them with suspicion before meeting them and didn't even get the name right as they referred to the man as Joe Vanelli.

We had not become acquainted yet when one morning a frantic woman carrying a little girl came running over to our house. She was almost hysterical as she pointed to a bloated bug stuck to the stomach of her daughter. She had never heard of a woodtick and this little bloodsucker had been busy. Mom was calm as could be as she said, "Don't worry; I can take care of it." We had a can of turpentine for such occasions and a drop or two on Mr. Woodtick was all it took to convince him to "drill out." It was the biggest, most ugly one I had ever seen and I understood their panic.

Mom and Adrienne introduced themselves and became close friends from that day forward. Cesare worked for the railroad; son John was seven and Paulette was five. They had moved west to escape the coal mines of Plains, Pennsylvania. Not only was the dust bad for a man's health, but the honeycombed ground beneath the town would periodically cave in, swallowing houses and the people in them.

They were great people and added a new dimension to our neighborhood. Cesare was a strong, hard worker and had come to the United States from Italy at age twelve. He could fix anything that was broken, constantly made usable things out of other people's throwaways, and helped his neighbors with all their projects.

They owned a rusty old car. Cesare found some cans of black paint in an illegal dump in the woods and decided it could be used to improve the looks of their car. The brush he had was way too small for the painting time he had, so he poured the paint into a pan and painted with a small broom. He seemed to have a nice touch, and it didn't look too bad, especially from across the street.

The next year, while we were looking for a Christmas tree in the woods, he found several cans of green paint; for months anything needing paint came out of their house pea green.

We went on many summer evening beach parties with them, usually to Silver Beach, east of town. This beach was clean, smooth gravel with about a dozen tall rustling cottonwood trees. We could have a campfire for roasting wieners and marshmallows and there was always a watermelon cooling in the lake. Those were indeed happy days.

Strangely enough, Adrienne didn't like Mom's name, Beulah. "Too old-fashioned," she said. Mom's middle name, Genevieve, was too complicated to suit her so she just called Mom "Jean." She didn't need a court order to change a name.

Our family stayed at two children, but the Giovenelli family soon outgrew their house and moved to a large two-story home at 1515 Montana Avenue. They eventually had eleven children.

Mandatory garbage collection was just coming onto the city law books and it was overdue. Some people preferred to go to the dump when they had a load, and some contracted with a garbage hauler for weekly pickup. The problem arose with the resident who casually tossed his garbage into a pile in his back yard and ignored it for months at a time. This contributed to the rat and mouse problems that plagued Coeur d'Alene both in the residential and downtown areas. We usually had a cat and, if Mom got stingy with cat food, we would often see the cat with two or three or more rodents in a day.

Cats love to show off and bat their catch around a bit before the kill. Once in awhile we would end up with an escaped mouse in the house, which made for lots of excitement.

The downtown movie theaters had rodent problems, and rumor was that a roving mouse would likely pick off a piece of dropped popcorn in midair before it hit the floor. The owner of the Roxy Theater, 115 South 4th Street, hired several cats to live in the theater and fix the problem. The cats thought they were in heaven as they knocked off mice right and left. They had way too many to eat, so they stockpiled them for future banquets. There is no smell quite like a dead mouse, so it wasn't long before this line of attack had to be abandoned and the cats were back on the street, looking to collect unemployment insurance. I now understand why the theater lights were always very dim, and the girl ushers carefully aimed their flashlights to help you get seated. They didn't want the theater patrons to see what was on the floor.

Back at school, our 8th grade teachers were all veteran teachers, and any student who cared to pay attention could learn a lot. Mae Lightheart, our English teacher, was a tiny lady who had no discipline problems whatsoever. She controlled with the

Bill Gundlach, Larry Strobel and Bob Cleveland with 8th grade diplomas.

tone of her voice. Math teacher Mary Laney had been a great teacher, but her health was failing and she was struggling. Some of the boys in the class took advantage, started shooting spit wads and discovered she didn't notice—even when they went "whap" against the paper roll-down shades. Paper airplanes crisscrossed the room. Then the hanging light fixtures began to get loaded up with wadded-up papers, candy wrappers, Milk Dud boxes and paper airplanes. The situation was out of control. Miss Laney gave up and retired in mid-year. The mild-mannered man who took over never did establish discipline; we really short-changed ourselves in the math area that year and paid the price in high school.

The night before 8th grade graduation the teachers put on an evening party/dance for us. I had a great time visiting, eating and drinking until Laura Masten asked me to dance. I didn't know how to dance, fell all over myself and ended up with a stomachache. I just hadn't arrived at the sophisticated and charming portion of my life yet.

After the graduation ceremony the next day Mom had a nice lunch party for Bob Cleveland, Bill Gundlach and me to celebrate receiving our diplomas. She took our pictures and it was a special day. That afternoon we rode our bicycles around Fernan Lake and went exploring in the Fernan Valley. We had a whole summer ahead of us and life was good.

4 High School

The summer of 1951 was a time of relief and happiness for having completed Junior High School. My excitement was mixed with apprehension as I contemplated becoming a high school student.

The many hours spent with Grandpa Stowe were already having a positive effect on me, but I didn't yet realize this. He had set such a good example that my work ethic was well-established, and I slowly began to understand that I enjoyed the accomplishments and satisfaction of physical labor.

My job as a *Spokesman-Review* newspaper carrier required arising at 5 am, folding the papers and hitting the road. No fooling around was allowed, as I was expected to be finished by 6:30 am. Conscience dictated that no paper be delivered anywhere but on a porch or in a newspaper box. Rainy days meant taking time to be sure all papers were placed in a dry place—no plastic bags in those days. I delivered about 100 daily and 150 Sunday papers. The papers for Monday through Saturday were sitting on our front porch when I woke up, but Sunday was different. There were so many "Sunday only" customers and the papers were so large that bundles of twenty-five were left on porches along my route. These bundles were distributed by the circulation manager during the wee hours of the morning. Darrell Robinson, a rotund, happy-go-lucky fellow, was easy to work for as long as we carriers kept our end of the bargain.

I had a large basket on the front of my bicycle—a replacement for the smaller basket crushed in the car door incident—that held the cloth "paper bag" nicely. I learned to backhand the folded newspapers so I could hit a porch from the street without slowing down. This sudden bombardment occasionally scared the wits out of a sleeping dog or cat and sometimes sent a milk bottle on a journey across the porch. Many households had milk delivered by a milkman and glass milk bottles with the name and address of the various dairies painted on them were the containers of the day. Delivering papers was usually fun.

I considered this to be a good job, better than working for the afternoon newspaper, The *Coeur d'Alene Press*, because a Press carrier had to interrupt his day's activities and ride his bicycle to the Press building at 2nd and Lakeside. Arrival by 3 pm was required to pick up and fold the papers on site and get instructions for new starts or stops for customers moving away.

The part of this I didn't like was collecting. Near the end of the month each carrier was required to knock on the door of every customer and request payment for the past month's papers. Some customers had the $2.00 for daily and Sunday papers in an envelope waiting for me. These good folks were a minority. Most people rummaged around in a purse, billfold, drawer, sugar bowl, cookie jar or some secret hiding place while I waited. A few complained loudly about the exorbitant price of the paper and some couldn't locate the paper card I was supposed to punch with my paper punch to prove they had paid. This was time-consuming, but I got the money eventually from most of them. The minorities at the other end of the scale were "financially embarrassed" and asked me to come back next week. It took ingenuity to collect from these people, but mostly it took perseverance. If I knocked on their door every day for a week or more, they would get sick of seeing me and finally pay. If I had the good fortune to catch them home when they had company, sometimes they paid to avoid embarrassment, and sometimes one of their visitors would pay. I considered this to be a big victory. The "dirty rats" who quietly moved away were the worst, as the carrier had to absorb the entire loss. The newspaper company didn't lose a penny.

Since my main job was done early in the day, time was left for lawn mowing, weeding gardens or flowerbeds, and window washing. Lawn mowing was done with an "Armstrong" mower, a mower that was pushed. The marriage of lawn mowers to gasoline engines had not yet taken place. Pay for mowing most yards was one dollar and there was no point in going fast. If I finished in less than one hour many people would have me clip grass or some other chore so that I spent a full hour to get the dollar. Like most fourteen-year-old boys I had dreams of buying a car, and if I didn't keep working I would never reach my goal—all my friends had the same goal.

Grandpa Stowe and I were spending a lot of time working together. His health was failing; he was bothered by shortness of breath and his feet were swelling. He insisted on raising his gardens as usual, but he needed more help. I was old enough to do significant work now, and some days I weeded and hoed by myself while he rested. I enjoyed working with him and now realize he was one of my best friends.

George Stowe hand-watering his last garden at 212 N. 18th Street. Summer, 1951.

Grandpa was such a thoughtful man and I never knew what he was thinking. One summer day Ralph and I were spending the afternoon with him helping with chores around his house when suddenly he asked, "Do you boys want to take a walk?"

"Sure," we answered.

We started north on 18th Street and Grandpa seemed to be walking rather stiff-legged, and I wondered what was wrong now. We crossed Elm Avenue and arrived at the boulder-strewn northern edge of the original Stowe homestead and followed a narrow trail into the woods. When we were out of sight of the road he pulled a 22-caliber rifle out of his left pant leg and said, "Your mother doesn't agree with me, but I think it is time you boys learn how to shoot a gun." He had never mentioned it before, but had obviously given the subject a lot of thought.

We got instruction first of all on safety. His eyesight wasn't very good, but that didn't mean he couldn't teach, as we received a step-by-step lesson in gun handling. Then he set up a target and we each had twelve shots. I couldn't seem to hit the target, but it really didn't matter; it was a fine and appropriate learning experience. Later in life I learned I must shoot left-handed for any semblance of accuracy.

Idaho law in 1951 stated anyone age fourteen or older could apply for and take a test to obtain a driver's license. Some of my friends already had their driver's licenses, so in August Dad decided I was old enough and he suggested we start my instruction. Driver Education hadn't been invented yet, so drivers' training was usually supplied by a family member. One evening after dinner Dad decided it was time for my first lesson. If our Plymouth had had a choice it would no doubt have run away from home. I raced the engine, let the clutch out too fast, and killed the motor over and over. Our poor Plymouth! When the engine didn't die, we hopped, jerked, and bounced before smoothing out. Then, it seemed, we would come to a stop sign and have to start over. It was a frustrating experience for both of us and subsequent lessons weren't much better. Two weeks of this ineptitude was enough to convince my usually patient father that I was not mature enough to drive a car. He promised we would try again "later", I was thankful I still had my bicycle.

September 1951 found me and my classmates starting high school in a three-story brick building at 7th Street and Montana Avenue, the same building my mother graduated from in 1928. This old, well-maintained building had a beautiful auditorium on the third floor and a serviceable gymnasium in the basement.

A running track circled the gym on the second level. The track team could run inside here during inclement weather, which happens frequently in North Idaho. There was a problem, however; the design engineers failed to notice the track was going to curve over the basketball court at all four corners of the gym and completely negate shots from anywhere near the corners. All shots from these areas were equivalent to shooting in a low-ceilinged room and the ball came back to the shooter almost as consistently as a boomerang. Needless to say, CHS was not developing any side shooters.

Heat for this building was supplied by a huge coal-burning furnace. In the morning, when it was fired up, giant clouds of black smoke belched from the chimney and engulfed the neighborhood in choking, foul-smelling coal smoke. Interestingly enough, nobody seemed to publicly protest and accepted this pollution as a way of life.

All freshmen boys spent considerable time and effort avoiding certain over-zealous upper-classmen who thought it was necessary to "initiate" us. The kids involved in sports took the brunt of this foolishness, but any 9th grader was fair game. I did a good job of being invisible and never got beat up. The teachers ignored this so-called rite of passage unless it led to bloodletting or broken bones on school property.

I remember other situations in the early 1950s that seem incredible 57 years later. When I managed to get myself in a little bit of trouble for a minor prank—some friends and I tipped over one of the last remaining neighborhood outhouses—I found myself with an appointment with Harry Spain, the local juvenile officer. While walking through the inner part of the police station on my way to Mr. Spain's office, I noticed three different desks had open bottles of beer on them. My session with the soft-spoken but eloquent Mr. Spain, by the way, was most beneficial in increasing my desire to behave myself and become a law-abiding citizen.

From his acre of garden on 20th Street Grandpa Stowe normally dug the potatoes twenty or thirty hills at a time and hauled them to his house in his homemade two-wheeled cart. Mid-October 1951 found him struggling with hundreds of hills still to be dug. He needed help, so Dad and I hooked the trailer to our car, spent a Sunday digging the remainder of his crop, and hauling them to his storage shed.

Several days later, when I stopped by his house after school, I found him angrily hosing off potatoes spread out on the ground near his woodshed. Times were changing and he didn't like it one bit. He had sold potatoes to McEuen's grocery store at 1123 Sherman for many years. Now they had a new produce manager and he had insulted Grandpa by refusing to buy unwashed potatoes.

"Any fool should know they keep better unwashed," he growled as he blasted water and rolled potatoes every which way. "The next thing you know they will want me to tie a blue ribbon around each one." It took a lot to rile my soft-spoken, even-tempered Grandpa. I was quite taken aback; I had never seen him show off his temper.

The changing times had caught up with him in other ways. He lived simply; but the expenses of electricity, water, clothes and groceries, plus property taxes, were more than he could make selling vegetables. He had always been self-employed, and had "retired" in 1935, without paying anything into the Social Security system. There was no social security check in his mailbox each month. This proud, hardworking, fiercely independent man had to apply for welfare. Each month he received a small check from the state of Idaho. This was assessed against his property so that, when he died, the state would recoup their money. This was a bitter pill for him to swallow.

Grandpa's slow decline was accelerated when he was forced to accept the heart-wrenching death of his oldest son, Bryan, who died suddenly from a heart attack in Portland, Oregon on January 30, 1951. Bryan was a typical Stowe—always willing to offer a helping hand. A neighbor, who was struggling with poor health, had a large load of sawdust delivered, and it needed to be shoveled through a basement window for future use in his sawdust-burning furnace. It was a typical rainy Portland Saturday. Bryan spent a good part of the day shoveling the sodden sawdust. By evening he felt ill. We received the bad news on Sunday and Grandpa took it hard.

As winter approached Grandpa's strength was slipping away. Dr. Howard Hughes said his heart was twice the normal size from so many years of strenuous labor, and his feet were extremely swollen. Finally, he couldn't live alone anymore and came to live with us. Dad set up a bed in one corner of our living room, and Grandpa was so weak he stayed in bed most of the time. Mom gave it her best shot, but Grandpa, as considerate and agreeable as he tried to be, wore her down and she became exhausted. As in so many similar cases, a good night's sleep was not possible. After ten days she couldn't do it anymore. None of his other children could or would take him in.

Dr. Hughes came to our house one late afternoon and kindly explained to Grandpa that he must move to "The New Home" nursing home at 1324 Lakeside Avenue. He objected vehemently. It was a heart-wrenching scene as Dr. Hughes led him to his car with Grandpa yelling, "No, no, no," over and over. We were all crying. It is difficult, even after all these years, to cope with this memory.

Every day after school I would hustle over to see him and we would visit. Without fail, something would trigger a memory from long ago, and he would soon be off and running on a story. He told fine stories and, true to form, many ended with a message meant to be beneficial to a teenager like me. The stories went along considerably faster without Uncle Charlie there to contest the dates of each event.

In the early morning of December 11, 1951, he peacefully passed on. Gone was a true pioneer, a man among men, who had worked long and hard to convert the North Idaho wilderness into producing farmland and orchards.

My life was changed forever.

Reverend Florence Cunningham, pastor of Church of the Truth, gave a sincere and heartfelt service for him at English Funeral Home at 411 Coeur d'Alene Avenue. I don't think he had an enemy in the world. The reverend remarked that many neighborhood children he befriended referred to him as "Grandpa Stowe." As this was the first funeral I had attended it was distressing to see my uncles, aunts and cousins sobbing. When we arrived at his gravesite in Forest Cemetery several inches of fresh snow made the footing slippery and dangerous. Uncle Charlie Williams, an emotional man in the best of circumstances, was having a wretched day. He was crying as he slipped and slid along leaning heavily on his cane to keep his balance. This prompted him to pronounce in a loud voice that he would die in the summertime so that his family would not have to endure cold and snowy weather the day of his funeral—a promise this man of good intentions was unable to keep. He died on January 4, 1953 when the weather was most unfavorable for a funeral.

We had a family gathering at our house after Grandpa's service; by mid-afternoon everyone had gone home. It was quiet and lonely and I was really moping around. I happened to look out my bedroom window and there was my friend, Bill "Willy" Gundlach, balanced on his bicycle as he leaned against our house. A few inches of snow didn't stop bike riders in those days. I went outside and he said, "I thought you might want to talk." It was one of his better ideas. We sat on the porch and had a lighthearted conversation, and I felt a whole lot better. Every fourteen-year-old would be mighty lucky to have such a friend.

I always felt fortunate to have so many uncles, aunts and cousins. Visits were pleasant and, after gasoline became plentiful with the end of World War II, quite frequent. Most of them were social folks who enjoyed visiting. Many Sunday afternoons would find up to three cars parked in front of our house. Dad would likely have a watermelon (in season) cooling in a tub of cold water and Mom would have a cake freshly baked. Before long, our house and yard would take on a holiday atmosphere with much laughter and spirited conversation. Sometimes we had a softball game; other times it was a checkers or Chinese checkers tournament for friendly competition. Grownups and kids played together and it was always a good time.

One of Mom's sisters, Aunt Ena, a well-meaning woman, had to be one of the most colorful relatives I can remember. When she was three-years-old lightning struck the corner of the Stowe ranch house near where she was sleeping in her crib. She wasn't physically harmed, but this violent incident left her emotionally damaged. She was jumpy, nervous and flighty, blinked her eyes rapidly, and her speech came out in machine-gun-like bursts. Her marriage to Oscar Brandvold was a study in opposites being attracted. He talked, walked and worked in slow motion, was unemotional, and never seemed to raise his voice or show anger. His personality was definitely "slow idle."

A visit by these two from Spokane always started with a sudden flurry of activity. Aunt Ena invariably leaped from their car as it rolled to a stop, made a dash for the house, usually startling our cat into scurrying for cover or racing up a tree. Our back door would burst open and slam against the wall as she flashed past and into the bathroom.

Uncle Oscar, meanwhile, slowly hauled himself out of the car, adjusted his hat and spectacles, and moseyed along at a snail's pace toward the house. This journey usually included an inspection of our flowerbeds and garden and some time to pet the cat if he had reappeared.

This gave Aunt Ena a five- or ten-minute head start on the latest news, which all too often concerned the latest escapades of their daughter, Joyce. She gestured wildly, batted her eyes rapidly and often ended up in tears. Uncle Oscar, meanwhile, looked for a chair as far away as possible from his wife and tried his best to find someone to share a quiet and relaxed conversation with him.

When their son, Roger, came with them we kids really had fun and almost always got into some sort of trouble. The bad news was—his idea of a little mischief tended towards destruction. However, he was a talented lad who could make flowers and vegetables grow beautifully, plus he played the piano well by ear. If he had ever heard a song he could sit down, pick around a minute or two, and then pound it out with embellishments. This was one of his special gifts in life, and the rest of the family could only shake their heads in admiration and applaud.

When it was time to leave, Aunt Ena hurried down the steps and was waiting impatiently in the car for several minutes before Uncle Oscar ambled out, got himself in and adjusted and slowly drove away.

We were individually either completely exhausted or soothingly relaxed, depending on the one we had spent our time with.

It was always a real treat when Uncle Gordon and Aunt Anna drove over from the Spokane Valley to visit. In fact, it was rather magical how a quiet, sleepy Sunday could rapidly be transformed into an exciting afternoon.

Uncle Gordon looked very much like his father, Grandpa Stowe, and had the

Gordon and Anna (Fishbach) Stowe; wedding picture, 1923. Photo courtesy of Lisa Gail Irwin.

Blackwell Lumber Co. sawmill. Closure in 1937 forced some families to leave Coeur d'Alene. Museum of North Idaho photo.

same kind, considerate and easy manner, along with a ton of enthusiasm and a great sense of humor. Life had not been easy for him, especially when his good sawmill job suddenly vanished with the 1937 closure of the Blackwell Lumber Company in Coeur d'Alene. After he found a job at a wooden box factory in Millwood, Washington they left their home at 816 Young Avenue and moved to E.8213 Euclid in the Spokane Valley.

The owner of the box factory took a real liking to his new employee. Gordon had the same innovative traits his father had, and as wooden boxes began to be replaced by cheaper cardboard boxes, it was time to change or go broke. Gordon's ideas led to new products soon being produced; under the name White Pine Sash and Door, they manufactured kitchen cabinets and even caskets, along with doors and frames. Near the end of the Depression business was poor, but Uncle Gordon never missed a paycheck as the owner made sure his best employee had a job.

Uncle Gordon was sports oriented. When he and Aunt Anna showed up we were soon happily batting a baseball, tossing a football or shooting baskets at our neighbors' hoop across the street. It always turned into a clinic; he had an eye for spotting any weakness in execution and was soon coaching us into better habits. Any game was a fun game with him around as his zest for life was infectious. He was such a livewire that we were sorry for the day to end.

Aunt Anna was a pleasant, laid-back lady, who kept busy much of the summer canning the bounty from Uncle Gordon's large garden. He had been Grandpa's best student, an expert gardener full of helpful hints for anybody who would listen. Their two children, Jack and Shirley, were grown by the time I was six or so, and my years of friendship with them came much later.

Uncle Jasper and Aunt Ruth lived east of town on the ranch where Grandpa and Grandma Stowe lived for so many years. The cherry orchard was still producing tons of pie cherries and I still worked there as a picker.

My cousins, Jasper Jr., George, Phyllis, Donna and Walter Hogeweide, were all older than I was, and I considered them all grown up because they were so capable and worked so hard at a variety of farm jobs.

Hogeweide family in 1945. Front, Ruth and Jasper. Back row, Walter, Phyllis, Jasper, Jr., George and Donna. Photo courtesy of Phyllis Hogeweide Swift.

Uncle Jasper was born in Holland and migrated to Canada when he was eighteen. He took a job as a lumberjack in the woods of eastern Canada and toiled ten-hour days to earn one dollar plus board and a tent to sleep in. Several years later he moved down to the United States and ended up at Coeur d'Alene because there were better-paying (though not by much) wood and sawmill jobs available.

Uncle Jasper was at times a noisy and brash fellow, opinionated and with a short fuse attached to a quick temper. Here we go again—opposites attract. Aunt Ruth was small, pretty and normally soft spoken. She quietly and efficiently worked steadily and was capable of turning out a mountain of work on a daily basis.

Their house was located in a long gulch on the east end of the ranch. There was not a view of the lake for the simple reason that their excellent source of water didn't come with a view. We went to their house fairly often so that Mom and Aunt Ruth could visit because Hogeweides still didn't have a phone.

When Aunt Ruth had bread baking in the oven of her wood stove, the smell was the best in the world, and I didn't want to leave for home. I knew that, if we hung around a little longer, the bread would come out of the oven and would soon be cool enough to slice. Thick slices with butter and jam quickly appeared for each of us. I hadn't thought much about heaven at that age, but was convinced that was about as close as one could get while residing on earth.

There was no end of work for the Hogeweides and each family member had assigned chores. There were chickens, pigs and several milk cows to be tended to and a large vegetable garden. Somehow Aunt Ruth, with some help from her children, had found time to develop an elaborate rock garden on the hill beside their house. It featured hundreds of various sized rocks and planted with every type of flower that would grow in North Idaho. She quietly worked with her flowers whenever she could find a few extra minutes, and this garden was the joy of her life. She was a calm, quiet woman and didn't say much until somebody requested a tour of her rock garden. Then she talked a steady stream of information about her flowers and plants: where they came from, when they bloomed, anything you could think of to ask. Her daughter, Phyllis, was her best helper, and student. In 2007 she still grew her own flower garden, providing bouquets of flowers for church each Sunday during the summer and fall.

As in so many farm households, there was no way to generate enough money to support a family no matter how long and hard they worked. Uncle Jasper worked at the Winton Lumber Co. Mill, later re-named Northwest Timber, located on the Spokane River at Gibbs, Idaho, a tiny community on the western edge of Coeur d'Alene. He and another man stood on a huge 20,000-pound machine called "the carriage" that resembled a flatbed trailer with equipment and handrails welded onto it. Built on six axles, the carriage rode on iron wheels that traveled on railroad tracks. Logs were rolled onto the carriage one at a time, and a man called the "dogger" controlled the large iron spikes "the dogs" that held the log tightly in place. The other man, called the "setter", Uncle Jasper in this case, kept busy adjusting the position of the log so the correct amount was slabbed off. Then the adjustment was made for the thickness of each board; this was done with a long handle connected to a big brass dial that held several rings with numbers on them, each ring for a different width of cut.

The carriage was controlled by the sawyer who sat in a phone booth-like structure, the sawyer's box, facing the carriage riders from the other side of the chain that carried the boards and slabs away. The sawyer was one of the most skilled employees in any sawmill and was paid accordingly.

The sawyer controlled the back and forth movement of the carriage, but his primary responsibility was to eyeball each log and make a mental estimate of how many boards of which dimension should be cut to produce the maximum board footage. Waste was bad—logs were expensive. The sawyer gave hand signals to Uncle Jasper so that he could make the proper adjustments. The amazing thing was that signals and adjustments, along with the log being mechanically flipped over, were done in a matter of seconds, and the carriage was moving the log right into the double-cut band saw that could cut boards coming and going. This had replaced the "old-fashioned" circle saw that could only cut as the carriage moved in one direction. The return trip, when using the circle saw, had produced nothing but a fast ride and sudden stop.

This whole operation was powered by steam. The steam pressure was controlled by a 44-foot-long cylinder, 12 inches in diameter, called a steam shotgun. The loud noise of steam being released was integrated with the screams of the saw as sawdust, bark, dirt and dust flew every which way. The men on the carriage didn't wear ear protectors or plugs, goggles or a hard hat. They did have gloves and sweat-stained old Stetson hats. They had a handrail to hold onto as they were thrown around like rag dolls by the rapid (and I mean RAPID) back and forth movement of this speeding monster. They did this with complete trust in the sawyer, knowing full well that a mistake or mechanical failure would slam the carriage into a huge bumper attached to the wall of the mill. If an accident did occur, the force could be intense enough to blow the wall out; and the carriage with its riders would end up outside. This would shut the mill down while repairs were made, and the company cast about for some new carriage riders.

I don't know how Uncle Jasper stood this kind of punishment year after year. Obviously he was tougher than nails and it didn't shorten his life much. He retired in 1958 and eventually lived to be ninety-five.

One day I got a firsthand experience of how it felt to ride a carriage. Mom took my brother and me to the mill to watch men and machinery work on several occasions, and as we stood watching, Uncle Jasper motioned for me to step onto the carriage with him.

"Do you want a ride?" he asked. (OSHA wasn't invented yet.) I nodded, "Yes," and within seconds I was wondering why in the world I had agreed. He held me in the crook of his left arm, and I held on to the metal railing for dear life as he constantly adjusted levers. We went so fast that my stomach couldn't seem to keep up with rest of my body, especially when the last two boards were cut, dropped onto the moving chain, and we zipped back to load a fresh log while not sawing anything. After a few minutes I had had enough and staggered back to solid footing. I discovered many years later that Walt Disney spent millions of dollars to develop a ride that produced the same sensation. Disney's ride, however, lasted only a minute or two. Uncle Jasper's ride lasted eight hours every workday.

Many mill workers tried this job, but lasted only a few days—weeks at best. They soon discovered that, even though they wanted the better pay involved, their bodies couldn't stand the physical abuse.

Our visits to the Hogeweide ranch were usually fun, but occasionally turned stormy. By all appearances Uncle Jasper ruled with an iron fist, and if anybody neglected an assigned chore, there was big trouble and he didn't care who witnessed the incident. He definitely had a kind and caring side as he did favors and was helpful to friends, neighbors and relatives. But, he made it plain that he liked to keep situations under his control.

One summer day, when I was fifteen, I was working at their place dragging logs out of the woods with a tractor to a small sawmill Uncle Jasper had built to saw lumber for family use.

Lunchtime was referred to as "dinnertime" at their house and was the big meal of the day. Jasper was uncanny in his ability to arrive at the kitchen door at 11:57 a.m., wash his hands, turn on the radio for the noon farm report, sit down and pick up his knife and fork just as the clock struck 12 noon. Aunt Ruth never seemed to miss her deadline, and the steaming bowls of food were delivered to the table at precisely noon.

This day was different. The clock struck twelve times and there was no food on the table. There he sat with his knife and fork and nothing to eat. He could have politely asked or he could have been patient. He did neither. He made a sharp-tongued remark about "no food on the table." Aunt Ruth whirled around from her position at the cook stove, pulled herself up to her full five-foot height, shot daggers with her eyes, and with a steady, clear voice declared, "You left the gate open, the cows tromped through my rock garden and flowers, and I spent half an hour getting them out. Dinner isn't ready because of your carelessness!"

I stared at my plate and silently cheered for Aunt Ruth. I had never seen anything like this. Uncle Jasper said nothing and seemed to be completely absorbed in the farm report that droned on and on with the prices of barley, oats, pigs, etc. It occurred to me then my soft-spoken Aunt had a lot more control than I thought; she had blown his image sky-high!

We didn't see Aunt Doris and Uncle John Gammel very often during my high school years. John had acquired an OK Tire Shop in Glendive, Montana. He had a knack for repairing cars and, combined with the tire business, had steady employment. Aunt Doris worked as a cook in a café and they finally seemed to be settled.

I missed having cousins MaryLynn and Janis around for visits as they were always fun, but Mom and Aunt Doris wrote so many letters we always knew what was going

The Fish Inn Tavern was a unique popular tavern at the east end of Wolf Lodge Bay. Museum of North Idaho photo.

on in their lives.

A Sunday trip to Uncle John and Aunt Mildred Strobel's house twenty-five miles east in the town of Rose Lake was always an adventure. We traveled on US Highway 10, which later was upgraded to Interstate 90.

Highway 10 was a narrow two-lane, curving and dangerous as the freight trucks and logging trucks lumbered along, holding traffic to a crawl. All too often an impatient driver would try an ill-advised pass and "crash!" another head-on accident that stopped traffic completely. We never had a wreck, but close calls were part of the trip. We always enjoyed seeing the Fish Inn, a unique tavern built at the east end of Wolf Lodge Bay. It was built to look like a giant salmon with a huge open mouth that was the front door. Another highlight was the tunnel at the summit of 4th of July Pass where Dad honked the horn repeatedly so we could listen to the echoes as we drove through. We turned south on State Highway 3, a narrow gravel road that zigzagged along the fence lines for several miles, before skirting the western edge of Thompson Lake.

The Strobel residence was a large two-story white house on a ridge between Thompson and Rose Lakes. The town of Rose Lake was about a quarter-mile farther south and was built on the northern bank of the Coeur d'Alene River.

A variety of logging equipment was always parked in their yard and a large garage/shop was several hundred feet north of the house. John was often working in his shop when we arrived, repairing and reviving his equipment. This was a great place to learn how welding was done, tires patched, and oil changed, plus some new words that Mom didn't want me to hear.

Wilbur Strobel—teenage truck driver, about 1940. Photo courtesy of Helen Strobel Chatfield.

Their house was usually a beehive of activity with friends and employees constantly coming and going. John always had twenty to thirty employees and several of them would, without fail, show up on Sunday afternoon on the pretext of friendly socializing. Then, on the way out, as a casual afterthought we would hear, "Oh yeah, while I'm here I might as well make a draw." (Big smile.)

Aunt Mildred would drop whatever she was doing, pad off to her makeshift office in one corner of the living room and write a check. Some of these guys made so many draws during the month that when payday came on the first of the month they had practically nothing coming. This financial merry-go-round never stopped and, though they worked hard, they were locked into inescapable poverty.

Sometimes there was entertainment. One Sunday Uncle John came hurrying in for dinner, slammed the back door just right and the window fell out. It made a frightful crash as shards of glass blew across the back porch. My cousins hooted and hollered and Cousin Jack yelled, "At last—something happened around here that Dad can't blame on us damn kids!"

John Strobel family; front row, John, Betty and Mildred, back row Wilbur, Helen, Walter and Jack. Photo courtesy of Helen Strobel Chatfield.

I swear these cousins, Wilbur, Helen, Walter, Jack and Betty, laid in the bushes watching and waiting for an opportunity for "payback." Uncle John fancied himself as quite a prankster and sometimes embarrassed his children. Helen was still working on payback from the first grade, for heaven's sake.

Her teacher, Merian Wick, often assigned a new spelling word to each student.

Come back the next day, spell the word correctly and earn a piece of candy. This was an innovative way to teach spelling, she thought. Well, it usually was.

On one occasion Helen drew the word "sure." After school she found her dad reading a newspaper in the living room and asked for some instruction with her new word. He spelled it carefully, and had her spell it several times to be sure she had it right.

The next day Helen was ready to earn her piece of candy. She raised her hand eagerly. "Sure—s-h-i-t," she spelled with conviction.

Teacher Wick couldn't decide whether she should laugh or cry. "And who told you to spell it like that?" she asked.

"My dad," answered Helen.

"I thought so," she said. "Children, please disregard Helen's answer. Her dad doesn't know how to spell very well at all."

No candy for Helen that day.

Sunday or holiday dinners at Rose Lake were consistent—the food was absolutely wonderful. There were sometimes unexpected situations, however, that almost got out of hand. One Memorial Day we made our usual visit to Lane Cemetery to place flowers on relatives' graves, and then stopped at Uncle John and Aunt Mildred's for dinner. The lilacs were in full bloom and Aunt Mildred's mother decided it would be nice to have a bouquet. She got rather carried away and ended up with a huge arrangement in the middle of the dinner table. She was real proud of her artistic contribution to a happy family event. We had barely gotten seated when Uncle John snapped, "Let's get this brush off the table!" as he jerked her masterpiece off the table and onto the floor behind his chair. By the look in her eyes and her body language, it occurred to me that Mrs. Bouchard just might go for his jugular. She didn't, but I'm sure he became more entrenched as her least favorite son-in-law.

Not far into my freshman year, Mr. Fahringer decided I had progressed enough to join the second violin section of the Coeur d'Alene High School orchestra. I sat so far back I was mostly hidden behind the stage curtain, but at least I was in. Ironically, the best violinist was Cookie Best and sitting next to me was Barbara Worst. Mr. Fahringer, always a taskmaster, came down hard on the older, more talented students. He never swore, of course, but when he became upset he would start a sentence with, "By thunder!" If a senior flubbed up he would say, "You will have to excuse him/her—that's a senior for you."

When he was really mad he would point his finger and yell, "Either get in or get out!" When this happened to some of the best players, I worried and fretted and wondered what was in store for me. As a concert approached he became grouchier by the day, but if someone bombed during a concert, he never scolded and never mentioned the incident beyond a passing comment, "So and so had a little trouble." For all his bluster I knew he was a deeply compassionate man.

During one concert a huge cymbal crash was required and at every rehearsal Jon Gellner, a fine, bold percussionist, would cut loose with a window-rattling crash. The night of the concert Jon reared back and went for it. Somehow the cymbals stuck together as if glued and all he got was a loud "whump!" His face turned fire-engine red, Mr Fahringer grimaced, and then smiled slightly. The next day he laughed about

Ray Fahringer in 1952, Coeur d'Alene School District Instrumental Music Instructor for 38 years. Photo courtesy of John Terris.

this embarrassing moment, commented that Jon had had the ultimate bad luck, and reminded us that the sun had come up that morning in spite of a less than perfect concert.

Then it was back to business as usual as we began preparation for our next performance. Music was high priority, but discipline was the ultimate concern in a Fahringer band or orchestra. He had his share of disappointments too. "Light Cavalry" was the featured piece at one concert. This composition features an exciting French horn solo near the beginning. He had a great horn section and thought it would go well. But on the night of the concert, for some unexplainable reason, the horn section seemed to lose their nerve with each player waiting for someone else to take the lead. After a couple feeble blats nothing else happened, and then it was too late. The next day he didn't really yell at them, but commented sadly, "If only even ONE of you had played it…."

The *Coeur d'Alene Press* was still an evening paper in 1952. In mid-April there was an article that surprised and stunned the community. Ray Fahringer was going to retire after thirty-seven years as instrumental music instructor for School District 271. The Rotary Club was planning "A Day for Ray" to pay tribute to his many years of producing outstanding performances with his band and orchestra.

May 6, 1952 was the big day. I was not a member of the band yet, so I watched the mid-afternoon parade at 9th and Sherman. Ray, his wife, Vera, and his son, Bob, rode in a Cadillac convertible with Mr. and Mrs. J. J. Broderick from Broderick Motors. The CHS Band was right behind the car and Mr. Fahringer kept looking back at them. Following were bands from Post Falls, Rathdrum, Wallace, Kellogg, Sandpoint and Lewis and Clark of Spokane with several drill teams among the bands.

A reception followed the parade at the "Penguin Room" of the Athletic Round Table in the Desert Hotel. Music teachers from all over North Idaho and Eastern Washington were in attendance, and many gave speeches and gifts. Glenn Exum, music supervisor at Kellogg High School, a legend in his own right, presented a gift and referred to Mr. Fahringer as the "dean of band music and directors in the state of Idaho." The Rotary Club presented the Fahringers with a large radio-phonograph combination.

The evening concert was at NIJC gym and was attended by 1800 people, twice the number of any previous concert. It was a great concert and I felt honored to be part of such a grand event as I sat at the back of the second violin section.

I was sorry to see him go, and worried and wondered who would be the new teacher. Then something unusual, unbelievable and wonderful happened. It was announced that Ray Fahringer would be teaching for one more year during the search for an appropriate successor. This made me and my orchestra friends wildly happy. Even though he was a strict taskmaster, we didn't want him to leave.

Coeur d'Alene of 1952 was doing well. There was no such thing as a mall, so the majority of the stores and offices were still downtown. The police station was in the city hall at 5th and Sherman, with the city jail in the basement below the police offices. The fire station was at street level in the rear of the city hall. All fire engines were at this location, and with the town growing, there was talk of moving to a more central location. It was exciting when the fire engines, with sirens blaring, roared out of the

Coeur d'Alene City Hall ca. 1925 at 5th and Sherman. Museum of North Idaho photo.

Coeur d'Alene Fire Department in 1936 at 5th and Sherman. Museum of North Idaho photo.

building and almost ran the cars up onto the sidewalk. One can still find the curved brick design for the firehouse doors on the east side of Cricket's Restaurant in Old City Hall.

Idaho First National Bank at 325 Sherman was the major bank. The Post Office was a fine-looking three-story building at 4th and Lakeside: The FBI and Federal Courtrooms occupied the upper floors. At the edge of the downtown area, the beautiful Kootenai County Courthouse building, including Sheriff's Office and jail, built in 1908, was located at 501 Government Way.

One of the most well-known business establishments was Dingle's Hardware at 402 Sherman, operated by T. Hedley Dingle and his son-in-law, Carter Crimp. This was an amazing store, and the rule of thumb was "If Dingle's don't have it, it doesn't exist." Just walk in and ask Mr. Dingle or Mr. Crimp for an item, no matter how obscure, and he would walk over to a bin or shelf and say, "It should be right about here."

One of the Sherman Avenue jokesters, the old men who sat on benches and visited, started a "rumor." The story was that Newberry's, a large Spokane variety store, was moving to Coeur d'Alene to merge with Dingle's Hardware. The name of the new store was to be Dingleberry's!

Friday and Saturday nights downtown typically provided an "old wild west" atmosphere. Slot machines and poker games were still legal with the Athletic Round

Kootenai County Courthouse in 1950 at 501 Government Way. Museum of North Idaho photo.

Looking west on Sherman Avenue from 6th Street, ca. 1940. Museum of North Idaho photo.

Table, Elks, Eagles, and Brunswick Cafe being the major players in the world of slot machines. Seymour's Cigar Store, Fritz's Corner, and the Club Cigar Store still had active poker rooms. Notable "rough" taverns were The Blue Jacket at 118 S. 4th (near the waterfront), and the Round Up at 115 N. 2nd. The Round Up still had sawdust on the floor, and their motto seemed to be "no matter what happens, don't clean it up—just add more sawdust." This made for a real old-fashioned authentic atmosphere, smell included.

Another interesting downtown business was the Coeur d'Alene Laundry, owned and operated by the Paul Schroeder family since 1922. This big gray building at 307 Front Avenue extended through the entire 300 block to the Roxy Theater building on 4th Street. In 1928 Schroeder's installed a central heating plant with a coal-fired steam boiler. Steam pipes were laid in the alley between Front and Sherman, extending from 3rd St. east to E.R. Elliot Ford at 502 Sherman. Also a pipe went north on 3rd to the alley between Sherman and Lakeside. It extended west as far as the Johnston Building at 123 Sherman and east from 3rd to a ways past 4th to service Rexall Drug, 112 N. 4th and the Wilson Building, 401 Sherman. An extension on 4th St. serviced the Montgomery Ward store at 119 N. 4th. Most buildings along the way tapped in for cheap heating until 1975, when the laundry was closed and torn down for the new bank parking lot. I remember many buildings heated with those heavy steam radiators, which were effective and clanked and banged when warming up or cooling down. In cold weather it was easy to pinpoint any leaks in the pipes as clouds of

Coeur d'Alene Lumber Co. in 1928. Lumber piles extended east to 8th Street. Mill site became the Coeur d'Alene city parking lot. Museum of North Idaho photo.

Coeur d'Alene Lumber Co. log storage in front of City Park and downtown area in 1920s. Museum of North Idaho photo.

steam seeped out of the ground in the alleys. The system was dependable except for a rare disastrous glitch when the laundry ran out of coal to fire the boiler during sub-zero weather.

Coeur d'Alene had another advantage for attracting shoppers to the downtown area. A several–acre free parking lot was available just south of Front Avenue between 3rd and 5th Streets. In Coeur d'Alene's earliest days this area had been a bay of Coeur d'Alene Lake.

The Coeur d'Alene Lumber Company started construction of a sawmill in 1900—nothing like having a mill at your doorstep. Advertised as the best plant in the state of Idaho; it could produce 75,000 board feet of lumber in 10 hours when nothing broke down.

When the poor economic days of 1929 forced the mill into closure, the city of Coeur d'Alene purchased this waterfront property for the bargain-basement price of $19,000. The problem, of course, was the needed cleanup. A sawmill creates a colossal mess over a 29-year period. This shallow bay site never was cleaned up, it was filled in; Coeur d'Alene Lake lost a bay and the city gained a parking lot.

The east end of the former bay was home to a horse racetrack for a time in the 1930s. On this site, called Mullan Park, cheap, quickly-built barracks-style apartments were constructed during World War II to relieve the critical housing shortage. After the war these buildings slowly deteriorated to the brink of slum status.

By 1952 there was talk of removing the Mullan Park buildings and using the land for tennis courts and baseball fields. Fortunately, this eventually came to pass. Mae McEuen was a driving force for this project and worked tirelessly to see it accomplished. On June 12, 1965 the city named the area McEuen Field and many thousands have enjoyed this public ground.

Further east between 7th and 8th Streets was a large ramshackle building called "the City Barn." It was home to all city street department equipment for storage and repair. Each year in early September the equipment was parked outside and suddenly it was the site for the Kootenai County Fair. There wasn't much room, but they had a little bit of everything a fair is supposed to have, including a midway of sorts on the west side that extended almost to Tubbs Hill. We always went and had a good time. The Fair was moved in 1954 to the vacated airport (Weeks Field) in the 4000 block of Government Way; the former hangar became the main Fair building.

In the wintertime the center of the City Barn was converted into a basketball court with temporary bleachers along the edges. It was cold and drafty and the lighting wasn't the best, but the CHS team liked it better than the high school gym because they could shoot corner shots, not having to contend with the overhanging track. This changed with the opening of the NIJC gym in 1949, which was a "great leap forward" for Coeur d'Alene basketball.

The City Barn lasted until the mid-1970s when it was replaced by the new City Hall, which was dedicated in 1978.

The Desert Hotel, 109 Sherman Avenue, was strategically positioned to afford a magnificent view up the main channel of the lake as well as unobstructed views of Kidd Island, Casco Bay and Cougar Bay. It was a major landmark in Coeur d'Alene, opened July 3rd, 1905, and built to resemble a California Spanish Mission. Originally

Typical load of logs on Sherman Avenue in 1950s before I-90 construction. Museum of North Idaho photo.

Desert Hotel ca. 1950. Museum of North Idaho photo.

named Hotel Idaho, it had one hundred rooms, cost $100,000 to build, and was advertised as the best hotel in North Idaho and one of the best in the whole state of Idaho. Victor Desert bought it in 1924 and renamed it the Desert Hotel.

The majestic tree-covered mountains and natural beauty were best seen from the south-facing rooms and, if you kept your eyes focused up and out, everything looked absolutely perfect. If your eyes picked up on what was staring back at you from ground level, it was a mind-boggling shock.

Directly in front of the hotel was the Milwaukee Railroad Depot, a long, weather-beaten wooden building badly in need of paint. Tall weeds grew all around it, and multiple sets of railroad tracks, plus short spur lines, extending toward the lake with a variety of parked boxcars provided the immediate lower view. Look a little farther and slightly left and there was Pointner's Iron Works. It was housed in a large battered metal building that had not been maintained for years. There were piles of scrap iron, barrels, worn-out machinery, old trucks, and mounds of just junk. It must have appeared to a hotel visitor to be the branch office of the city dump. Look past Pointner's and there stood a line of over-mature cottonwood trees, some partly fallen with hanging dead branches. Some had already collapsed and lay rotting on the ground. The water's edge oozed oil from the long-ago days of the boat builders and the water was full of old timbers, boards and tons of scrap metal carelessly discarded into the lake during the last fifty years or so.

A pier jutted into the lake at the foot of 3rd Street and logs were regularly dumped into the lake from railroad flat cars. The log booms weren't all that unsightly, but the tons of bark and debris floating around weren't exactly picturesque.

The foot of 1st Street featured a lengthy rotting pier that had been the electric railroad termination point during the early part of the century, where the passengers stepped off the train onto a steamboat for a lake cruise. The lake beyond held an unsightly collection of half-sunk houseboats, rotting docks, abandoned machine shops and boat shelters, half- submerged logs, decaying pilings and stumps.

Here we sat on the edge of a lake, famous for being one of the five most beautiful lakes in the world, and we had a mess of gigantic proportions. It was a disgrace slowly developed over years of thoughtless behavior during the boat-building years and straightforward neglect since the 1930s when the steamboats disappeared.

Nobody seemed to know where to start, but change was coming, and it would be impressive beyond my imagination. The man to eventually trigger this transformation would be Bob Templin.

There were many ways to describe Coeur d'Alene during this era, but it was foremost a lumbering community.

In addition to the large mills, numerous small mills were scattered throughout the area. Some were owned by farmers who sawed logs from their own property for their personal use. Most obtained logs from nearby ranchers and landowners, sawed them into rough boards and sold them to one of the large mills, where they were dried and planed into finished product. This created more profit than selling logs to the big mills.

Madson's Box Factory at 2003 North 3rd Street found it economical to buy timber, hire a logging crew, and run their own mill adjacent to the box factory. This

Coeur d'Alene waterfront ca. 1950. Cluster of buildings in center background is Mullan Park, built as emergency wartime housing. Museum of North Idaho photo.

Dozens of logging trucks traveled Sherman Avenue each day in the 1940s and 1950s. Museum of North Idaho photo.

Potlatch Forest Sawmill at foot of 23rd Street, our neighborhood mill. Museum of North Idaho photo.

Potlatch was a major lumber producer in Coeur d'Alene, Idaho. Museum of North Idaho photo.

mill provided material for wooden boxes widely used for many things grown and manufactured.

The major mills all had steam whistles that blew, signaling the beginning and end of shifts. The sound of the mill whistle at Potlatch Forest, located on the waterfront at the foot of 23rd Street, was part of my life each work day. My early memories included times when the mills ran out of logs in the wintertime and Dad had no job. When the mill whistle was silent we had very little money.

When the mill whistle blew, it meant men were working hard at jobs that paid a living wage and their wives could stay home and raise the children. It was a sound of comfort, announcing all was right with Coeur d'Alene and the world.

Typical sawmill steam whistle. Photo courtesy of Paul Hakala.

As a young person growing up I was expected to keep track of time by paying attention to the whistle that blew at 7 a.m. and 11 a.m., noon, and 4 p.m. There was usually a night shift marked by whistles at 4:30 p.m., 8:30 p.m. and 9:30 p.m. plus 1:30 a.m. When the mill whistle blew at 4:30 p.m. it was my cue to head for home, tend to chores, and go to the grocery store if Mom needed anything. If I was late she scolded me saying, "Didn't you hear the mill whistle?"

When my sophomore year in high school started, I was one ecstatic kid. During the summer I had been the recipient of a miraculous growth spurt—long overdue—and the first day of classes was really fun. Some of my classmates didn't recognize me and thought I was a transfer. Wow! This did wonders for my self-esteem. Larry Cleveland, Bob's dad, made the statement that he would no longer refer to me as "mouse meat." I really hated that name and this was a relief. He kept his word.

If a girl is small she is called cute: but when a boy is small he is an automatic target for disrespectful and cruel comments. A year before, as an example, we were visiting Uncle John and Aunt Mildred one Sunday at Rose Lake and I was having a pleasant day until I walked through their kitchen and encountered one of their neighbors who had dropped by to chat. I heard her ask Mom, "Is that your boy?"

"Oh, yes," she answered.

"And how old is he?" was the next question.

"He's fourteen as of last March," replied Mom.

"Hmmm, mighty puny for his age, ain't he?" was her less than kind observation.

I was hurt and embarrassed, but was too shy and polite to comment on the fact that her fanny hung four inches over each side of the poor old chair seat she was parked on.

So at school I was feeling very good, but more was on the way. I accidentally did something right and enrolled in a speech class. The teacher was Earl Priddy, a tall, distinguished-looking gentleman who was kind and soft-spoken. Thanks to him my life was about to change. About a third of the class was seniors, so the atmosphere was more serious and mature (from a sophomore point of view), and I thought students like Frank Delevan, Sally Barrett and Jo Ann Noble were quite sophisticated.

Mr. Priddy taught us to write and deliver speeches. His practical approach was just what we needed as we practiced making introductions, shaking hands and holding doors open for ladies. We were taught to be helpful, kind, gracious and considerate. I had been painfully shy, had little knowledge of social graces and a glaring lack of self-confidence.

He convinced me I could stand up in front of a roomful of people without fear or nervousness and deliver a speech that included eye contact to every area of the room. He insisted we never start our speech until we had the complete attention of our audience. I am still benefitting from those lessons of 1953.

About two months into my sophomore year Mr. Fahringer stopped me in the hall and said, "You are doing pretty well in orchestra. Do you want to be in the band? I would like you to learn baritone horn or mellophone."

The mellophone was often referred to as a "peck horn," but for reasons I don't remember, I did pick the mellophone. It was fairly easy to learn and my violin ear-training was a big help. The Fahringer policy was to reward string players an easier job in band so they could participate in parades and football field shows.

The Coeur d'Alene High School Band uniforms were blue and gold, very prestigious, and had been purchased for the band by the Athletic Round Table. I was thrilled and honored to be with the older boys and girls in the band, even though I only played a raspy-toned peck horn. I didn't know this banged-up old instrument was to be a big stepping-stone for me.

In the spring of 1953 Dad was teaching me (again) to drive. We went chugging around town in our 1938 Plymouth as my shifting skills improved and I quit killing the engine at every stop sign. It was great. I didn't bump into anything either.

The big day came. Dad waited while I took the written test. It was easy to memorize the rules and regulations and I got 100 % on that part. Then a tough-talking deputy named Elmer Muller went with Dad and me while I drove. He did his job well, was very serious, and lectured me sternly about the merits of being a careful teenage driver. I only killed the engine once and got lucky as I did a real nice parallel parking job. So I got my driver's license and, like most teenage boys, started thinking seriously about buying a car.

The day of Mr. Fahringer's final concert was approaching. He had held the same job since 1915 and was an institution. To hold the position of instrumental teacher and conductor for thirty-eight years at the same school was highly unusual. If there was anyone more well-known and respected in our town, I sure don't know who it was. We all realized that stepping down would be difficult for him.

My lukewarm attitude for band and orchestra had been improving, and I knew that without the frequent "kick in the pants" from Mom I would have been a dropout. Now I experienced an attitude adjustment; suddenly my goal in life was to make Ray Fahringer proud of me. Perhaps I was growing up and maturing a little bit.

The band rehearsed Monday, Wednesday and Friday, and the orchestra rehearsed Tuesday and Thursday. Many of us played in both groups. We prepared carefully for the final concert of the Fahringer regime.

The concert was scheduled to be held in the NIJC gymnasium, the only place in town large enough to accommodate the expected large crowd. The big day approached, and plans were made for school buses to transport us to NIJC for dress rehearsals.

The band played first and went through a crisp, high-spirited rehearsal. We were ready and we were good. The ride back to the high school was noisy and jubilant.

The next day the orchestra had their turn. The orchestra was a smaller, more tightly-knit group that practiced and played with more concentration and emotion than the band. On this day it was a happy rehearsal as Mr. Fahringer quietly fine-tuned our playing. It seemed to be a magical hour as we made the final preparations.

At the conclusion of rehearsal, we presented him with a new fishing rod and reel and a Pendleton jacket. It was then that I saw the real Ray Fahringer for the first time. He talked to us quietly, and even though the room felt super-charged with emotion, he kept his composure as he chose his words slowly and carefully. It was so quiet that a dropped pin would have been heard by all. It occurred to me that surely the clocks of the world had ceased to tick and time was standing still.

He was completely humble as he explained how much we meant to him. He commented that his strict discipline was meant only as a method to develop our toughness so we would be better prepared to succeed in life. "There are only two ways to do things," he said, "the right way and the wrong way, and you need to be able to recognize the difference." Then he informed us he considered us the "cream of the crop." It was a quiet bus ride back to the high school.

The concert was excellent and we all knew we had experienced something profound. He would no longer be part of my daily life, which was a negative. I had no idea of the friendship that would eventually develop between us, and that he would become a major source of positive influence and guidance until his death twenty-seven years later. In fact, he is still part of my life. How many times do I ask myself, "How would Ray handle this?"

I had been saving money from my various jobs; so in the summer of 1953, before my junior year in high school, Dad and I started looking at cars. Then, as now, there was a lot of iron out there. We finally found a 1946 Ford four-door sedan that appeared to be in good shape. After visiting with the former owner, Orville Wright, I decided to make the purchase of my life up to now. I shelled out $385 for this beautiful maroon vehicle; a mighty serious investment for a sixteen-year-old in 1953.

My first stop, of course, was at the State Farm Insurance office at 735 4th Street. Agent Lloyd Henry was jolly and congenial as he got me all fixed up with a policy that cost me $15 for the first six months. He left the typing and safe-driving lecture to his wife, Meryl.

As it turned out, this car was a good investment and it ran well except for one fault. If I worked it hard summer or winter and the engine got hot, it would vapor lock. This was typical of many Ford V-8s of the day. The only remedy was to wait until it cooled off, and then it would start and run fine. If I was in a hurry, the car didn't care. This little quirk didn't keep me from taking it on "long trips" to Sandpoint, Spokane, Worley and Kellogg.

CHS played its football games at Persons Field at 15th and Garden. One of the best things about owning a car was to go early, drive onto the track encircling the football field, and watch the game out of the weather in comfort. A carload of friends piled in and we all cheered together.

Late in the summer, while at a private violin lesson with Ray Fahringer, the new band and orchestra director for Coeur d'Alene High School walked in. When I was introduced to Gilbert N. Burns as "one of the best students you will be getting," I almost fell over. I didn't think I was playing very well yet.

Gil Burns was a tall man, about 6'3", big-boned, balding, and he wore rimless glasses. He was cheerful, friendly and just bubbled over with enthusiasm. He had played in and conducted military bands, grown up in Coeur d'Alene and was a former Fahringer student.

Soon after school was underway I observed his style of teaching was in sharp contrast to the Fahringer strict discipline methods; but we all had to respect his musical ability. Indeed, he did know how to teach music. All we had to do was keep quiet and pay attention.

Not far into my junior year I decided I really wanted to move on from the mellophone and play French horn. I badgered Mr. Burns until he came up with a horn for me, and I started to practice with enthusiasm. Before long I knew this was where I belonged in the musical part of my life as I became enthralled with the horn and its sound. My progress was steady, and by spring of 1954 I played part of Mozart's Horn Concerto No. I at the Solo and Ensemble Competition in Lewiston. To my surprise, I received a superior rating.

Mr. Burns bought some woodwind quintet music, and I became a member of this group, which included Andrea Whitla, flute, Gertie Carder, clarinet, Curtis Nelson, bassoon, Carol Jackson, oboe, and me on French horn. We were soon in demand for meetings, teas, graduations, parties, dinners and even played on television in Spokane. This was a good time in my young life, and I felt that I belonged somewhere and was achieving a goal—Ray Fahringer obviously was proud of me. Many of my friends were involved in athletics, but I was too small and slow for any sport. Band

Gilbert Burns, new instrumental music teacher, fall of 1953. Photo courtesy of Janet Best Haakenson.

Larry and Ralph Strobel ready for a CHS band concert in 1953.

and orchestra gave me the boost I needed to stay focused on school.

A lot was happening in the spring of 1954. A new high school was under construction in a former hayfield at 15th and Hastings. Our long-time high school building at 7th and Montana Avenue was scheduled to become part of the Junior High complex; there would now be a north building to go with the existing south building. Our class of 1955 would be first to graduate from the new school and this was exciting.

During the spring of 1954 I started dating my first girlfriend. Peggy Weller was also a horn player so we had a common interest. She was a good pianist as well; but her real specialty was pantomime, which she performed at many functions. The Wellers lived on a farm at Mica Flats and Floyd worked at the Kaiser plant with Dad. Peggy's mother, Margaret, with brothers Bill, Larry and Clyde with sister, Diana,

Coeur d'Alene High School Band in 1954.

Coeur d'Alene High School Orchestra in 1954.

made up an all-American family.

We went to dances at Mica Grange Hall where I learned to square dance and round dance. We tried to steer clear of the rowdy, noisy kids who hid beer in gunnysacks in their cars and sneaked out to drink when nobody was looking. We had a lot of fun, but as is usual with most teenage romances, we went our separate ways after going steady for a while.

One of the best activities available during my high school years was the popular weekly teenage Friday night dance in the Eagles Lodge at 209 Sherman Avenue. The dance was always upstairs in the large ballroom/lodge room where the small door to the west of the main entrance opened to a long stairway. The doorman was usually Bert Booth. There was no charge; but if you appeared to have been drinking you didn't get in.

Local unionized adult bands played live music, often Gus Best with his group. They were good. Wayne Sullivan was the bouncer, a pleasant, big-boned wide-bodied fellow who was strong as an ox. He was known to pick up misbehaving boys by the shoulder using only one hand as he carried them to the top of the stairs and bade them farewell.

Most of the girls were good dancers, but only a few of the boys got on the floor. It was crazy. Most of the boys milled around and visited on one side of the room while the girls stood and visited on the other side, gave up waiting for the boys, and girls danced with other girls. I wasn't much of a dancer and stood around and missed the opportunity to improve. It was a safe and orderly place for teenagers to congregate and have a Coke or 7-UP. If you left, you couldn't come back in until next Friday.

The Eagles Lodge deserves many thanks and much appreciation for all the years they sponsored the teen dances.

The summer of 1954 was special because I was awarded a scholarship from the Coeur d'Alene Rotary Club to attend a three-week music camp at the University of Idaho in Moscow. I had excellent instruction for both violin and horn. When I played a horn solo for a talent show I stood up to play. The next day, one of the instructors told me, "It is as appropriate to sit down and play horn as it is to sit down and play cello." Not all hornists agree, but it was a point well taken, and I do agree and have followed that bit of advice all my life. I met some really nice kids at camp, and one of them, Doug Klein, became a lifelong friend.

Bob Cleveland was working in the Coeur d'Alene City Park that summer for the "Old Pro" of yard work, Avery Shadduck. Bob gave me some tips he had been taught and my yard skills improved. That led to work in some nice yards around town with "word of mouth" my only advertising. I did extensive weeding, trimming, spading, edging, etc. for the Berg family at 801 South 11th Street. When they wanted a tree cut down, I talked Bob into helping me. We took Dad's cross-cut saw, dropped the tree across the driveway and sawed it up. For us, this was a major accomplishment and we learned what hard work was all about.

This was the summer my friends and I started calling each other by a middle name or nickname. Gene Branson became Charlie, Bob Cleveland was Bennie, Bill Gundlach was Bump and I was Georgie as some examples. This was good for a little confusion and we thought it was great fun. Some of my high school friends stayed in the Coeur d'Alene area and have been like extended family through the years.

My senior year of high school started late. The new high school at 15th and Hastings wasn't finished; we didn't start classes until the third week of September AND we didn't have to make it up! The two side-by-side buildings still weren't ready, but we moved in anyway and shared space with the carpenters and finishers. The connecting breezeway and gymnasium had not been built yet. The place looked like two warehouses sitting in a muddy field, and it was pretty tough going outside across the field to a class in the other building. When the fall rains came, that old hayfield was so soft that the unpaved parking lot became a big mud hole. Cars parked there sometimes sank to their axles and had to be extracted by wreckers using a long cable. The floors were as muddy as a barn some days and mud became a way of life. I don't think the school board envisioned anything like this.

There was an "all-purpose" room in the middle of the south building where the choir, band and orchestra rehearsed. The home economics class used the room part of the time, and meetings, assemblies and pep rallies all convened in this large, busy room.

About a month into this crazy school year, somebody had the extremely poor judgment to vandalize the boys' restroom. Principal Harold Evans called all the boys into the all-purpose room for an assembly and when the red-haired principal stood up to address us he was so mad even his hands were red! "This school isn't even finished yet and somebody is tearing it apart," he shouted at us. "If this happens again, I'm going to padlock the rest room door and have an eight-hole outhouse built at the far end of the parking lot, and that will be where you'll be going the rest of the year."

I idly wondered to myself what kind of permit that would require, but wisely refrained from asking. There was no more vandalism, so the guilty party must have believed him.

One of my most interesting classmates was Graydon Johnson who lived with his family on a farm at Meadowbrook, about two miles west of town. Graydon was tall, blonde with a crew cut, ready smile and a twinkle in his eyes. His best friend was Loren Murphy who was shorter, good-looking, with a black-haired crew cut. This dynamic duo was bright, curious, inventive and mischievous. They kept busy with scuba diving, sail boating, ice boating (a sail boat rigged up to travel on the frozen lake in winter) and a steady stream of pranks. They had a cider press they used to process apples in the fall so they could produce their well-known hard cider.

Geiger counters were suddenly popular in 1954, as quite a few people were busy exploring with these machines in hope of finding uranium. Most of us, however, had heard of them, but really didn't know a Geiger counter from a bean counter. One morning I got to school early and there was Graydon, hanging out in the hall, carrying a wooden box about five inches square. He was waving around an aluminum-covered wire shaped like a pistol that came out on one side. Six or eight other students, including Loren, were loitering in the general vicinity.

"Hi Graydon," I said, "What is that thing?"

"Haven't you ever seen a Geiger counter?" he asked. "This is the latest invention for finding uranium, you know."

I looked at it with curiosity and he waited patiently. The nearby students weren't going anywhere, but didn't appear to be paying attention either.

I didn't know how painlessly easy it was to be set up as an unsuspecting victim.

"Well," I asked, "How does this thing work?"

"Oh, let me show you," he said, with a big smile.

"You just take this pistol thing and point it at your wrist watch," he instructed, "and I will give you a demonstration."

As soon as I had the pistol in my hand I briefly heard a buzzing sound, and I took a jolt that just about blew my hat off. I jumped and yelled right on cue, and those milling-around students were howling with laughter. Come to find out, they were all former victims, enjoying themselves as I fulfilled my duty as a future victim making the smooth transition to present victim. The box contained only a D cell battery. Graydon had it rigged up so that when he pressed a button on the bottom of the box it sent an electrical current into the pistol. There was only one thing to do. I joined with the other former victims, and followed Graydon around as he jolted everybody he could lure into his trap. It was great fun after the initial introduction, and it was good for about two days before word spread throughout the school. He thought long and hard about zapping a teacher or two, but never quite had the nerve.

Graydon had spent considerable time perfecting this little prank. He was way ahead of the average student in his understanding of terms like magnetic fields, induction coil, high current-low voltage and electrical flow. Physics teacher Ed Specht fretted constantly that Graydon would accidentally electrocute one of the other students with an experiment or prank.

Behind his big smile, Graydon's sense of humor was always working overtime. Georgia Finch was a good friend to both Graydon and Loren. She lived with her

Louie's In-N-Out, teenager hangout. Museum of North Idaho photo.

family in a large, rambling Fort Sherman-era house on West Lakeshore Drive. One hot summer evening Graydon phoned Georgia and invited her to go to Louie's In-N-Out at 608 N.W. Boulevard for a milkshake. She agreed to go and soon heard an engine outside. To her astonishment, Graydon was tooling up their driveway on his dad's farm tractor.

"Ready to go?" he asked with his best smile.

The shock of a red 1950 International Harvester Farmall tractor at their front door was taken in stride by the Finch family. Georgia, good sport that she was, hopped up onto the implement hitch behind the seat, put her arms around Graydon's waist and hung on for dear life. The hitch was a long, curved metal bar with a flat surface, so the footing wasn't too bad for an agile teenager. Neighbors and motorists along the way were pointing, laughing and honking as the tractor slowly moved along toward Louie's. Graydon's sense of humor had hit a home run this time. The girls at Louie's drive-in window were appropriately shocked and entertained, but recovered well enough to mix a couple of shakes.

Graydon parked the tractor in the big lot between Louie's and the Feed & Seed farm store where everybody parked their hot rods and family sedans to enjoy their food. This parking lot was always busy as teenagers compared engines, talked horsepower, paint jobs, wax and chrome cleaner. Not a one of them was prepared to talk about a Farmall Super C rig that boasted a 21-horsepower engine. How did they know this

The Boat Drive-In at east end of Sherman Avenue—the favorite teenager hangout. Museum of North Idaho photo.

kid wouldn't lower the tractor bucket, slip it under their car frame, and flip them over if they insulted him? Some of the hot-rodders quietly idled away and drove to the Boat Drive-In, run by Hap Murphy, at the other end of Sherman.

Graydon had pulled off the ultimate, harmless prank and entertained many Coeur d'Alene folks along the way.

As I mentioned earlier, Mom and the majority of the women we knew canned many jars of fruits and vegetables every summer to get us through the long winter months. The idea of a freezer in every home hadn't taken hold yet and most people couldn't afford one anyway.

In the 1940s and 1950s lockers were popular to freeze and store meat, fruits and berries. Most men here hunted to provide meat for their families and needed a place to store it after it was cut and wrapped. In 1954 there were several cold-storage lockers listed in the City Directory, including Cowles Cold Storage and Lockers at 1117 N. 8th St., East End Lockers at 1200 Sherman, YJ Meat Packing and Cold Storage, on the side of the old Brewery Building at 612 Mina and Cy's Meats and Lockers at 1324 5th Street.

Coeur d'Alene Brewery Building housed YJ meat-packing and cold-storage lockers. Museum of North Idaho photo.

They charged a small monthly fee for a locker, affordable to most. The lockers were often built in conjunction with a meat market and consisted of a large room full of rows of various-sized enclosures resembling rabbit hutches. Each "box" was numbered and had a door with a hasp for a padlock. The bigger the "box" the more it cost per month.

The room was refrigerated right down to about 0 degrees. If Mom had me stop by Cowles Lockers on a summer day to pick up something from our locker it required some planning, which I usually did not do. Say it is 85 degrees outside and why would I have a coat with me? I went in with padlock key in hand and tried to hurry. The sudden change in temperature was not very conducive to hurrying because I was soon shaking so bad I had trouble getting the padlock unlocked. Then I had to find the requested items on her list and nothing was in any particular order inside the locker because the frozen packages were all mixed up by the last family member to be there—hopefully not me. That person had been freezing and was also in too big a hurry to be tidy. So I would plow through the various shapes of frozen packages, read the labels rapidly, and do my best to get out without frost-bitten extremities. Sometimes I got so cold I would go outside, warm up, and then take another run at it. Occasionally I would quit acting like a dumb kid and arrive at the locker with coat, hat and gloves.

This system had one noteworthy flaw. During July and August the huckleberry pickers hit the woods and many people decided to freeze part of their picking; this was okay as long as the berries were packed in glass jars. Sure as shooting, someone who had no jars or was uninformed would use paper or cardboard containers. WOW! The huckleberry smell would about stop you in your tracks when you next entered the locker, and some people claimed their steaks and hamburger suddenly had a huckleberry flavor.

In the late 1950s home freezers became popular, and within a decade locker boxes went the way of the iceman—the end of another era.

At the start of my senior year Gil Burns recognized we had a real decent French horn section, so he bought some quartet music and coached us some days before school. Lynn Schwindel, Peggy Weller, Sharon Carkuff and I were soon doing a creditable job. Suddenly, it seemed, we were in demand with invitations to play for all sorts of gatherings—gratis of course. It was during this period I discovered that playing while the audience is eating is pretty much a lost cause. It is just too hard to compete with mealtime chatter, clinking glasses and clattering silverware.

Our woodwind quintet was going great guns also, so I was getting lots of experience performing in public. My senior year, the quintet consisted of Shirley Horning, clarinet, Curtis Nelson, bassoon, Warren Anderson, flute, my brother, Ralph Strobel, oboe, and me. We had great fun and were well-known.

My brother, Ralph, started studying clarinet in the sixth grade, and it soon became obvious he had a much greater aptitude for music than I did, as he made fast progress. He ended the eighth grade playing very well and Gil Burns had just lost his high school oboe player to graduation. He brought an oboe to our house for Ralph to practice on during the summer as an experiment. This was a perfect fit and his progress was spectacular. When school started in the fall of 1954, Ralph was ready to handle the oboe parts for both band and orchestra.

Ralph soon discovered what all oboe players discover: it is difficult to buy good reeds. He checked out a book at the city library and read up on reed-making. Oboes require a double reed, which is difficult to make and play. Then we went to Spokane and bought tools and supplies. His first attempts netted nothing but frustration with reeds soaking in little water containers sitting on windowsills all over the living room and kitchen. One day, unbelievable as it was to me, he got one to work. He stayed

CHS Woodwind Quinted 1955; front row from left, Shirley Horning, Curtis Nelson, back row, Warren Anderson, Larry Strobel and Ralph Strobel. Coeur d'Alene Press photo, courtesy of Warren Anderson.

with it, and suddenly he got it right and produced a real beauty. This was cause for great jubilation and relief at our house.

Ralph took his new reed and went to his private lesson at Ray Fahringer's house. He started playing and Mr. Fahringer said, "Say, you've got a darned good reed there. Where did you buy it?"

"Oh, I made it myself," Ralph casually replied.

Mr. Fahringer was in no mood for any foolishness. He glared at Ralph and snapped, "Don't fool around with me, Boy, where did you get that reed?"

"I made it," Ralph insisted.

Ray Fahringer had to back up and start over that day, and he soon had new respect and wonder for this 9th grade boy.

"If you can turn out good reeds consistently you can sell all you want," he advised.

Eventually Ralph developed a thriving mail-order oboe reed business and this supplied part of the money for his college education.

One day, well along in the fall of 1954, Gene Branson met me at the door as I got to school. He told me there was a lost hunter, and if we volunteered to go and help search for him, we could skip school, but still get credit for being there. We quickly decided this would be more of an adventure than going to classes, so we hustled over to the office and signed up.

We had until 10 a.m. to go home, change clothes, pack a lunch and meet at the Eagles Lodge. The lost hunter was a 65-year-old retired miner/farmer named William Honey. Five of us young fellows rode in a car with James Barrett in a convoy of cars and trucks to Cocolalla Lake, where Mr. Honey's car had been discovered. Mr. Barrett told us about Mr. Honey as we drove along, and I felt proud to be involved in the search for such a fine man as he described. I knew a lot of people, but had never met the Honey family.

A base camp had been established near Cocolalla Lake, a beautiful gem about thirty-five miles north of Coeur d'Alene. A big fire was burning and coffee and snacks were available. Lots of people were coming and going—obviously Mr. Honey was well liked.

We spent the rest of the morning combing an area south of his abandoned car. No sign of him. While we were eating lunch, a very upset Mrs. Honey came along, talked to us and thanked us for being there. She was afraid her husband was alive and suffering somewhere in the cold, wet woods. Many of his friends were spread out, looking in all directions, but had found no trace of him.

After lunch, the search organizers lined the whole works of us up on the road—a line at least one-half mile long— and we went north. We were told to walk straight ahead through the brush, detouring only around trees. We were only about ten feet apart and men with walkie-talkies were spaced throughout the line to help keep the line straight. It was a slow, but intensely thorough search. Almost an hour later we were a long ways into the woods and the old man next to me was grumbling that a hunter as old as Mr. Honey would never have gone this far from the road. Waste of time or not, we kept going because nobody could think of anything else to do.

Suddenly the man on my left said, "Oh, oh, there he is," just as my eyes focused on a man's body clad in a red and black checked coat. He had fallen forward with his rifle under him, his hands still clutching the stock and barrel. He had not suffered—death had come instantly.

Someone shot into the air three times to signal the search was over. Searchers cut two saplings, coats were stretched between them to make a stretcher, and we took turns, six at a time, carrying the body back to the base camp. Mrs. Honey and her family had gone home and an ambulance was waiting. It was dark when Mr. Barrett got us back to the Eagles. I was upset—I had never seen a dead body except at a mortuary.

When I read the obituary later, I noticed a surviving granddaughter was named Sharon Spain, and I idly wondered if she was any relation to Harry Spain, the Juvenile Officer who had lectured me about my evil ways after the outhouse tip-over incident.

My senior year was without question my most successful year of school. Gil Burns wasn't too enthused about attending all the basketball games so he gave me a little instruction in the art of baton waving and turned me loose, masquerading as "pep band student director." This was great fun and a real confidence builder. I realize now I didn't really know what I was doing, and probably proved this band didn't need a director to function. We had lots of fun, entertained and added excitement to the games, and that was what we were supposed to do.

One day during band rehearsal the door to the all-purpose room opened slightly, and a hand dropped a mouse on the floor. The poor confused mouse ran straight for the band and many of the girls started screaming. Mr. Burns hadn't seen a thing, but when some of the girls were suddenly standing on their chairs, he decided he had better stop conducting and check out the problem. The rehearsal bleeped and blatted to a halt, and Mr. Burns was completely baffled by the fact his rehearsal had turned to chaos in just a few seconds.

The mouse ran past my chair and I leaned over and caught it. I took it out into the hall, and there stood a known prankster, Dick Shoemaker, obviously enjoying the screams coming from the female band students.

I made a lucky guess.

"Here's your mouse, Dick," I said, and handed it to him. He didn't say a word, just took the mouse and hurried off down the hall.

I was the big senior hero that day because I caught a poor, harmless, scared-to-death mouse. I had heard rumors that women sometimes stood on chairs if a mouse ran across the floor, but I had never before witnessed this phenomenon.

In the fall of 1954 I had applied to become a member of the All-Northwest Band to be convened in Eugene, Oregon in the spring of 1955. Much to my surprise, I was picked to be one of the four first horns. Two orchestra members, violinist Carol Pederson and cellist Bettina Scott, were chosen for the All-Northwest orchestra.

Finally the day came to leave for Eugene, and Mr. Burns loaded the three of us into his big, comfortable, easy-riding, gas-guzzling Packard. It was a wonderful car that could pass anything except a gas station. Mr. Burns was a good driver in most ways, but we soon discovered that he had a problem keeping up with stop signs and red lights while driving in unfamiliar territory. We sailed through a stop sign in Portland and luckily got away with it. A few miles down the road we zipped through a red light right in front of a police car and that was a problem. We were pulled over immediately.

"Oh, my gosh, did I go through a red light?" exclaimed Mr. Burns. "These three giggling teenagers must have distracted me."

The stern-looking officer instructed us kids to help our teacher watch for red lights, and he wrote a warning ticket. A few blocks later a green light turned yellow and we all yelled, "STOP." He stopped with a screech, but was too far into the intersection. He hastily backed up and promptly forgot to shift back to "drive." So when the light turned green we backed up some more which set off frantic horn-honking behind us. We didn't bump into anything, and thankfully escaped Portland unscathed.

I should insert here that Gil Burns was one of the kindest, intelligent, most well-meaning men I have ever known, and he would never have purposely broken the law or caused any trouble. He was a little distracted sometimes, and was known to come to rehearsal with his pants buttoned to his shirt because he forgot his suspenders, and we could tell he always slipped the knot on his tie. Nevertheless, he did an excellent job programming and directing the band and orchestra and his marching band routines won many awards.

In Eugene a boy from Eatonville, Washington and I were housed with a very nice family. The lady took us to and from rehearsal, and cooked wonderful meals for us. Instructors for the All-Northwest band, orchestra and choir were top-notch, and I learned a lot. The concert was attended by a sell-out audience and this experience was the highlight of my musical career so far.

Mr. Burns organized a string quartet that year and included Carol Pederson, violinist, Lind Karlson, violist, Bettina Scott, cellist, and me on violin. My violin playing had improved a lot, but my real musical interest had shifted to horn. Mr. Burns must have been worried I might have a few spare minutes each day, and he asked me to take up drumming for his newly-formed dance band. This was a tough project since my sense of rhythm hadn't developed much yet. I had trouble hitting the right things at the right time as my right foot did bass drum while my left foot did high-hat cymbals. I finally got my hands and brain fairly well-coordinated with my feet because Mr. Burns just wouldn't give up on me. I learned a little bit about percussion and this would prove to be beneficial later in life.

For the Lewiston Music Festival in the spring of 1955 I tackled Mozart's 3rd Horn Concerto and once again received a superior rating.

The Class of 1955 was blessed with many fine teachers. One who impressed me was Ray Stone. He taught U.S. Government, a class I took my senior year. The subject matter sometimes became secondary as he attempted to prepare us seniors for the rigors and pitfalls of the adult world. He related to us his experiences as a football coach in a small central Idaho town. When his team won Friday night, he was everyone's pal when he went downtown Saturday morning. When the team lost, the same people crossed the street in mid-block to avoid speaking (a study in human nature). He stressed the importance of honesty and fairness and became furious when he discovered one boy baited a substitute teacher by telling her his name was Fletcher Decker, a notorious town drunk of the time. That was a form of abuse, he said, and was not acceptable.

Mr. Stone told us college was important and desirable, but some of the happiest men he knew worked at a sawmill or mine and had relaxed evenings to take their kids fishing, sledding or skating. He went out of his way to become acquainted with us as individuals and encouraged our special interests.

The last day of class Mr. Stone told us, "I am going to bid you goodbye with some advice I want you to remember. Moderation is the key to success." It was good advice and I have always remembered it. Not to say, however, that I always remembered to follow it!

Time sped by and suddenly the CHS Class of 1955 was practicing for graduation. Our class numbered about one hundred fifty, and was unique in that we had five sets of twins: Tom and John Richards, Janis and Joyce Adams, Marlene and Darlene Bjaaland, Joe and Jim Hensley and Donald and Dorothy Heyn. Principal Evans decided the five sets of twins would lead us as we marched into the gym. This was all the more appropriate because the Richards twins were valedictorian and salutatorian.

Graduation night was busy for me because both the woodwind quintet and the horn quartet played as part of the program held at the NIJC gym, the only place in town large enough to accommodate the crowd. For me, it was an exciting and fulfilling evening in all respects.

Larry Strobel; graduation picture in 1955.

There was no organized all-night celebration for the seniors in those days, so there were family parties and a few ill-advised get-togethers, including one at the Clark House on Hayden Lake featuring "beer in the woods." Fortunately, all our class members survived. As for me, I bought a milkshake at the Dari-Delite, 1224 Sherman Avenue, and drank it slowly and thoughtfully as I sat on our front porch and pondered the future. I had my diploma, high school was over; but beyond the excitement was the realization the security blanket provided by School District #271 for the past twelve years was gone.

Now what? Basically, I was happy and optimistic, but it was time for making decisions and planning the future. Did I want to go to college, and if I did what goals did I wish to pursue? Did I want to get a permanent job? There were numerous job opportunities, thanks to four major sawmills, Potlatch Forests, Northwest Timber, Atlas Tie and Ohio Match. They were successful and ran two shifts every day of the week. Kaiser Aluminum, located in the Spokane Valley at Trentwood, was a major employer that ran three shifts daily. The Silver Valley—Kellogg, Wallace, Mullan area—had numerous mines and a smelter. A job was available any day of the week, as there seemed to be an ongoing shortage of mine workers. If you could pass the physical, you were in.

Some of my friends were starting their working careers immediately, as they followed their dads to a sawmill, mine or retail store. Dad said he could get me a job at Kaiser Aluminum if that was my choice.

I had lived in Coeur d'Alene all my life. Did I want to stay here? A few of my classmates couldn't wait to leave. Kyle Walker, our one-man Chamber of Commerce, traveled extensively promoting Coeur d'Alene with lectures and slide-shows. After attending one of his programs, it occurred to me how lucky I was to be living in such a fabulous place!

We had so much here that was enjoyable—the bustling downtown, city park with so many huge trees, the exciting baseball and softball games at Memorial Field and great basketball at North Idaho Junior College. Playland Pier, built on a filled-in portion of lakefront at the east end of City Beach, had a carnival atmosphere. There was a merry-go-round, Ferris wheel, bumper cars, loop-the-loop, swings that swung out over the water, penny arcade games, and lots of food, including cotton candy. We had camping, fishing, hunting, hiking, boating, skiing and best of all, our beautiful lake.

To my knowledge, the best hamburgers in the world were served right here in Coeur d'Alene at the Missouri Lunch (later Hudson's Hamburgers), owned and operated since 1907 by the family of my classmate and good friend, Roger Hudson.

Conclusion: I loved living in Coeur d'Alene and, YES, I wanted to stay here.

My first plan of action was to get a job. I had wanted to work in the woods all my life and now seemed to be the right time to give it a try, gain experience and further my education in the world of logging.

5 Summer of 1955

As I mentioned earlier, my uncle, John Strobel, lived at Rose Lake—a little one-tavern town twenty-five miles east of Coeur d'Alene. He was a logging contractor and worked for one of the major sawmill operators of the area, Russell and Pugh. They would buy a Forest Service timber sale and Uncle John's job was to see that the trees were cut and the logs delivered to their mill.

One Sunday, shortly after high school graduation, Dad and I were visiting Rose Lake and I got up enough nerve to ask Uncle John for a job. He hesitated a bit. "Okay," he said. "I still have a season to go on that timber sale up Fishhook Creek above Avery. Want to live in a logging camp? I'm sure I can find something for you to do."

I was excited. Avery was so far out into the woods I had never even been there. All my life I had been fascinated by logging and the equipment involved. As a young boy, whenever we visited Rose Lake I would go out in the yard, crawl up into the seat of a logging truck and pretend I was driving a loaded truck out of the woods. I'd sit on the seat of the bulldozer and pretend I was building a road. I daydreamed of cutting down trees, watching them crash to the ground and then cutting them into logs.

Uncle John knew, and I didn't, that I was as green as proverbial grass when it came to woods work. He was too kind to say so. He was six foot two and big-boned with broad shoulders. His head was large with close-cropped hair, a long Romanesque nose, a ready smile and kind eyes. He was a true gentle giant.

He told me, "You will need to go to White's in Spokane and buy a pair of caulked boots." Caulked boots pronounced "corked" were custom-made heavy leather work boots that had about fifty little nails sticking out from the sole and heel. This made for no-skid walking and kept a logger from sliding off every log he stepped on.

He probably hoped I wouldn't buy the boots, but I did. I had to pay thirty dollars for them, which was a considerable investment for me.

Uncle John was a man of his word, and in early June he called me and said, "The snow has melted, and the mud is drying up. I'm getting ready to open the camp. Want to go to work Monday?" Boy, did I!

I drove my trusty maroon-colored four-door 1946 Ford to Rose Lake on Monday morning. I was so excited to be going to a job in the woods I could hardly sit still. I helped Uncle John load his pickup truck with various supplies that needed to be taken to camp.

Uncle John had been one of my heroes since childhood; I sensed it was a good time to get better acquainted, and we did. As we drove through Kellogg and Wallace, famous mining towns, he pointed out the buildings of numerous mines and told me their history. In the town of Osborn he showed me a long row of nearly identical houses and explained that they had all been moved from Rose Lake after the sawmill burned and wasn't rebuilt.

We left Wallace after buying two dozen cases of canned food and drove up Placer Creek toward Moon Pass. We passed the mine where Ed Pulaski, a well-known firefighter, had taken shelter with his crew during the 1910 fire. That had been the largest, most devastating fire in the history of North Idaho and had burned for two months. These men had huddled in this sweltering mine as the fire raged outside and most lived to tell about it.

This part of Idaho and its history were all new to me, and I loved it. The views from Moon Pass were spectacular. Mountain range after mountain range loomed before us clear into Montana. The air was fresh and clean and there was no sound except the wind in the trees.

We descended into a long valley. The remains of huge, burned-out cedar trees covered the valley floor. This was how a magnificent forest looks after a fire. It had been forty-five years since they burned, and they still looked like an army of huge grotesque creatures reaching for the sky.

The road was narrow, dusty and bumpy, but according to Uncle John it was a great improvement from past years. We followed the Milwaukee railroad tracks the last ten miles into Avery. Uncle John explained how these rugged Bitterroot Mountains had looked like a giant anthill when thousands of Asian laborers worked with picks, shovels, wheelbarrows and dynamite. There were seven tunnels and a huge trestle on this ten-mile stretch. It had taken a superhuman effort to engineer and lay track here.

We arrived in Avery, a town of about two hundred permanent residents. It was nestled in the bottom of a narrow mile-long canyon and looked to me as if it would be perfect for filming a movie circa the late 1800s. As we entered the east end of town I noticed a long row of small, dusty, weather-beaten houses tucked against the rugged mountains on the north; each had a woodpile on the front porch or nearby. The valley widened slightly and we came to a brick powerhouse (electric substation), a three-story hotel with a wide front porch, a railroad station, fishpond, post office, Avery Mercantile and grocery and a gas station. Several tavern/restaurants were wedged into the remaining spaces. The Forest Service ranger station was perched precariously on the mountainside. The town was busy with people coming and going in every direction. This was an isolated but functional community. The mercantile sold a little bit of everything including food, dry goods and tools.

At least half of the canyon floor was covered with railroad tracks. This was a switchyard where locomotives lined up the boxcars in the desired order. Some would go east over the mountains into Montana and beyond. Some would travel down the St. Joe valley to Spokane, Washington and points west.

The St. Joe River took its share of the canyon floor. "Beautiful" was the right word to describe this swiftly flowing river of pure, clear, clean water.

Several locomotives were busy pushing boxcars on the tracks and hobos sat in the open doors of some of them. We crossed a high bridge over the tracks and river. On the south side of the canyon we passed the school and several nice houses. Then the setting changed into a jumble of strange little cabins and trailer houses jammed close together with all kinds of clutter, wrecked cars and woodpiles scattered everywhere.

Avery, Idaho was located in a remote one-mile-long narrow canyon on the St. Joe River ca. 1955. Museum of North Idaho photo.

Down river, back on the north side, I could see a long, flat area where several cranes were loading logs onto railroad flat cars fitted with upright stakes to keep the logs from rolling off.

We soon came to a ramshackle board building with a crudely painted sign identifying it as "Sam's." Uncle John pulled in and parked.

"Time for lunch," he said.

We started in, and I was holding back a bit. I told him, "Uh, this is a tavern and I'm only eighteen."

"Don't worry about it," was his answer. "There ain't any law in Avery." Nobody paid me any attention so I relaxed.

Sam's was a simple enough place with a bar along one wall, a small dance floor, and tables and chairs placed everywhere else. The floor was all chewed up from caulked boots and hadn't been swept of late. I decided the place could politely be called rustic.

The waitress came over and Uncle John casually said, "We'll each have a T-bone steak. What do you want to drink, Larry?"

Since I had never drunk a beer in my life, I couldn't order one of those, but to say "milk" in this place might be quite embarrassing. I said it anyway. I was very relieved when, to my surprise, she didn't laugh or even smile. And then there was this business of a T-bone steak. Lunch to me, if I didn't have a homemade sandwich, was at best a hamburger and milkshake. I knew Uncle John liked to eat, but this was incredible.

"This is quite a day," I thought. "I am learning a lot in a hurry here." Little did I know!

The steaks came with all the trimmings. The cook knew what he was doing for sure. The place might look like a dump, but they could put out food. It was delicious.

We were nearly finished eating when the door opened and in came a pretty young woman. Obviously, the Avery Mercantile didn't have too much selection in clothing. This poor girl had gotten stuck with a blouse and jeans that were two sizes too small. I heard silverware clatter to the floor somewhere behind me. Uncle John gave her his full attention and watched her intently as she sauntered up to the bar and adjusted her very shapely bottom onto a bar stool. He turned to me, smiled slightly and winked. He didn't say a word. My education was moving into high gear.

We were soon driving up Fishhook Creek on a narrow two-lane dirt road with turnouts. The creek roared out of a very narrow canyon with sheer rock walls and steep hillsides with trees miraculously hanging on wherever their roots could take hold. This was the road built and maintained by Potlatch Forest Industries, a large wood products company, to access vast areas of forest near the headwaters of the Clearwater River. We met a loaded log truck before long and I was shocked. Here came a Euclid truck with a load twelve feet wide. The usual maximum width is eight feet. Euclid built the biggest trucks in the world, which were usually used for earth moving equipment. This monster had a load that reached for the sky. John whipped into a turnout, giving the truck driver all the room he could as the truck went thundering past us. I had seen these trucks being used on highway construction, but never dreamed of anything like this.

Potlatch had built this road and could do anything on it they wanted. Normal rules did not apply. The uphill traffic had to stay on the creek side at all times, and the downhill traffic (loaded trucks) stayed against the bank. There were "stay right" and "stay left" signs directing you where to go and where to be and, if you didn't comply, you could be squashed like a bug by the next Euclid. This road was quite new and maintained with great care. It was graded smooth as a table and watered constantly. An old fellow with a wide pitchfork walked the road all day and threw every rock, limb, piece of bark, and pebble out of the way.

Early-day loggers harvested trees off the steep hillsides for about three miles up Fishhook Creek. At that point the creek bottom became a box canyon, a giant dead end. The creek went out and around a massive rock formation and tumbled through a narrow gorge. The only way to extend the road was to tunnel through the mountain.

In the mid-1930s several CCC (Civilian Conservation Corp) crews were assigned to the St. Joe River in the Avery area. One of the projects to be tackled was blasting a tunnel to open up the Fishhook drainage. This turned out to be the largest St. Joe Forest project attempted by the CCC. Often two shifts worked, and on a good day they moved forward eight feet. When finished they had used ten tons of blasting powder in 2,227 holes to create a tunnel 415 feet long, 20 feet high and 24 feet wide. The rock is so solid that no bracing or concrete work was required.

Potlatch had the inside track for timber sales in this area and built Camp 44 to house loggers and their families close to the logging operations. It looked like a small Idaho town, only much neater and better organized. It had a little store and a nurse on

North entrance of Fishhook Creek tunnel near Avery, Idaho blasted through solid rock by CCC crews ca.1938. Museum of North Idaho photo.

duty in case somebody got hurt.

Three miles up the road from Camp 44 was Uncle John's camp. Russell and Pugh Lumber Company, thanks to a fluke, had managed to purchase a Forest Service timber sale adjacent to all the Potlatch activity and had contracted Uncle John to log it. His trucks hauled the logs twenty miles to Avery where they were lifted from the trucks directly onto railroad cars. This sale straddled the ridge separating the Clearwater and St. Joe drainages. The water on the south side of the ridge flowed into the Clearwater River; the north side flowed to the St. Joe River.

We pulled into Uncle John's camp in early afternoon. This camp consisted of three bunkhouses, a cookhouse, wash room/shower house, Uncle John's little trailer house and two outhouses. The buildings had board floors and board walls four feet high with the remaining wall and roof areas covered with tent material. The tent part came off for the winter so the deep snow wouldn't cave in the buildings.

Each bunkhouse had a wood-burning heating stove, and the cook tent had a large wood-burning cook stove. The camp was located in a natural bowl with a small creek running through adjacent to the cook tent. The ground was muddy between the buildings, so twelve-inch wide boards had been laid across the soggy places.

There was a parking lot on a small hill above the camp, out of the mud. A five hundred gallon gas tank to fuel the equipment sat on a metal stand. Two of the bunkhouses were large enough to sleep eight, but Uncle John took me to the smaller one that had four beds. I took a look around and the first pangs of homesickness hit me.

"What am I doing here?" I thought. Here I was, a hundred miles from home. I suddenly longed for the familiarity of Coeur d'Alene.

In the area between the parking lot and the first bunkhouse somebody had sawed a large buckskin tamarack tree into blocks about fourteen inches long. Buckskin, in this case, meant the tree had been dead so long that the bark had fallen off. Uncle John grabbed a new axe and a metal hardhat out of his trailer and we went over to the woodpile.

"You'll be the bull cook," he said. "That means you're the camp handyman and Jack-of-all-trades. I need some signs painted, but for now I need a bunch of wood split. Keep your hardhat on and show me you are good enough with this axe to not break the handle." I could split wood—I had lots of woodshed experience.

A little past three o'clock the various crews started coming back to camp. I had bought black jeans, blue work shirts, wide black suspenders, and, of course, my shiny new caulked boots. I hoped I looked like I belonged here. Most of the loggers were muddy and looked tired. A couple stopped and introduced themselves, but most just ignored me as they plodded to their bunkhouse.

I was a slight five feet nine inches tall and weighed all of one hundred and twenty-five pounds. To make it worse, I wore glasses. I doubt anybody was impressed. I noticed there were some really rough-looking characters among them, and I began to feel a lot more homesick. I carried a supply of firewood to each bunkhouse and stacked it handy to the stove. It was quiet. All the men were flopped on their beds either dozing or reading.

At the cook tent (everybody called it the "cook shack") I met Stella Smoots. She was fiftyish, heavyset, with a pleasant face and a cheerful, friendly voice. I felt better as she welcomed me in and told me where to stack the wood. "Bring me lots," she said. "I start baking about three in the morning."

Uncle John had mentioned her during the ride up. "She doesn't move fast, but she never makes a wasted motion," was his comment. "And she is one fine cook!"

The previous summer he had had cook problems. Most logging camps did, it seemed, but Uncle John had gotten himself into a rather unlikely situation. He had hired a woman originally from Arkansas, an "Arkie," and she chewed tobacco all day. Her custom was to lift the lid of the cook stove and spit into the fire. That wasn't too bad, but she all too often, in her haste, cut loose a big blast of juice, timed it wrong and dropped the lid before its arrival. This resulted in a "Sssszzz" sound as it skittered across the hot stove. When the smells of cooking food could no longer camouflage the smell of sizzling tobacco juice, he had let her go.

Stella made me feel at home. She explained that I would need to dig a hole at least one hundred feet down the creek to bury the garbage so the bears wouldn't come around. She asked me a few questions about myself and I knew I had made a friend and felt a lot better. Maybe this would work after all.

So far the only other occupant of the bunkhouse where I was staying was Clyde Peterson. He was about six feet tall, balding, very thin, with a bony face that seemed almost emaciated; but he had well-developed arm muscles. When he spoke, I was astounded that this gangly-looking man could have such a deep, well-modulated voice; it was quite melodic, and he seemed so friendly and sincere that I liked him immediately.

Dinnertime was five o'clock. Stella had a triangular metal "dinner bell," and when she was ready, she whacked it a few times with a short metal rod. The "boys," as Uncle John referred to his crew, came to life in a flash. They bolted out of the bunkhouses and went charging into the cook shack like a runaway herd of horses. When the dinner bell rang—look out!

The cook shack was set up with long wooden tables with wooden benches on each side. The heavy-duty ironware plates and the silverware were hopelessly mismatched and probably came from secondhand stores. But who cared? The crockery bowls of food started at the end near the stove. The food disappeared out of the bowls like some sort of magic act. The empties were passed back and a full one came in a hurry. There wasn't much conversation except, "Pass the spuds," "Pass the gravy," "Pass the bread," etc. I noticed, with humor, that sometimes when a fellow at the far end of a table asked for something, there were so many men helping themselves along the way that he received an empty bowl. That was good for a curse or two, but not to worry, there was plenty of food. I had never eaten anything better, with the possible exception of the lunchtime T-bone, and here we had cherry pie for dessert.

Uncle John liked to eat and his crew reaped the benefit. Some days he would drive down to Avery on some pretext and return with a treat such as whipping cream. "Thought you boys might like it," he'd say. The motto seemed to be "What John eats, everybody eats."

Breakfast was also served in the cook shack. On the way out after breakfast each man stopped at a table near the door and made his own lunch from a nice array of sandwich makings plus cake, cookies and coffee. Three dollars for three meals per day were deducted from our checks at the end of the month. One dollar for this kind of meal was the best deal in North Idaho—maybe even in North America.

Right after my first supper in camp, Uncle John told me he needed me to go back to Rose Lake with my cousin Jack. He needed the log trucks and drivers to come up to camp the next day. A fellow logger, Savvy Procoppio, had a shortage of trucks and had offered John a good deal if he would haul some of his logs. His camp was a few miles up the road, so it would not be inconvenient to haul his logs.

I was to drive Uncle John's new Ford pickup back the next day, following Jack and two other drivers in the big White trucks. What a day this had been!

"I must be doing okay," I thought, "if Uncle John will trust me with his new pickup."

I liked Jack. He was eight years older than I and had been kind to me as we grew up. He was married to a pretty Italian lady, Barbara, and had two children. He was a big-framed man, not much taller than I was, but twice my size and very strong. He wasn't fat—just big.

A favorite family story was that he had once picked a pesky, unwanted door-to-door salesman up by his collar and the seat of his pants and lifted him over their picket fence onto the sidewalk. His departure was rapid enough to leave rubber marks on the street.

Early evening came as Jack and I started back down the Potlatch Road. We stopped near the Camp 44 dump and watched three large brown bears looking for their dinner. These were the first bears I had ever seen in the woods. Somewhere between Wallace and Osborn two deer bounced across the highway and Jack narrowly missed them.

We arrived back at Rose Lake and I was mighty tired. Aunt Mildred said I could bed down on their living room sofa and I fell asleep immediately. After what seemed like forty-seven seconds, Jack was shaking me awake. It was still dark. What was this?

"Gotta go," Jack said. "Dad didn't get around to licensing the logging trucks yet this year and we've got to get them to the St. Joe River road before it gets light and the cops are around. Once we get on up towards Avery we'll be all right because there isn't any law at Avery." Seemed like I'd heard that before. "Hurry up!" he coaxed. "It's already two o'clock."

"So there really are two two o'clocks in the same day," I thought as I fumbled and stumbled into my clothes.

Jack, Carl Anderson and Dick Moyer rumbled out of the yard in the trucks and headed south on State Highway 3. I followed in the pickup.

I was wide-awake now and I noted with interest that the logging trucks were equipped to haul ten-foot-wide loads. That was two feet beyond legal for this highway. Then I noticed there were no clearance lights to indicate just how wide the trucks were. We rounded a curve, and I could see that the two front trucks were minus the red glass on the lone taillight. No mud flaps either. "No wonder we are doing this in the dark," I thought. "If this little caravan gets stopped by the State Patrol, he will be writing for an hour." Uncle John's bank account would take a very hefty hit.

It was uneventful to the St Joe River road. Nobody was around. Traffic was nil. I felt really pleased to be driving Uncle John's pickup.

They parked the trucks a little way up the river road in a wide, dark place and piled into the pickup with me. This approached a circus act, but we made it. "Time for breakfast!" yelled Jack as he tried to get the door closed. Carl Anderson sat next to me, then big Jack and the smaller Dick Moyer sitting on his lap with Dick's head bumping the roof.

We didn't have to go far into the logging town of St. Maries. It was only 3 am, but an enterprising restaurant owner was open. I was hungry now, and ready for a logger's breakfast of eggs, bacon, hash browns and a pancake. What a great breakfast!

As we prepared to get back into the pickup, Jack looked up and down the street and remarked, "I hope there are no cops around. If they see us shoe-horned into a rig like this, we're in trouble."

Everything looked peaceful and quiet. A big black-and-white cat appeared on the curb nearby, looked dutifully both directions, and scampered across the street. Nothing else moved. Except for half a dozen loggers eating breakfast in the restaurant, the town was asleep.

I was used to parallel parking in Coeur d'Alene, but here in St. Maries diagonal

St. Maries, Idaho, a prosperous logging town on the St. Joe River, ca. 1950. Museum of North Idaho photo.

parking was the custom. With diagonal parking you are expected to back out the way you drove in and, if you wish to go back the way you came, you go around the block. It was only 4 am, and I didn't see any harm in backing out and making a big swooping arc as I crossed the street backwards.

We headed back the way we came, but about 111 feet into the return trip, we noticed flashing red lights behind us. Police cars were still equipped with red lights in those days.

"Oh, God!" moaned Jack. He was well known for his cussing ability, but this sounded more like a prayer. I stopped, of course, rolled down the window and waited. A St. Maries police officer came bustling up, and he looked extremely mean-tempered. He sounded even meaner.

"What in the HELL kind of driving was THAT? You got a driver's license, kid?" While I was squirming around trying to reach my billfold, he shined his flashlight into the cab. I swear his eyes bulged out an inch.

"What in the HELL are you guys doing?" he bellered. By then I was trying to explain my backing maneuver.

"I live in Coeur d'Alene," I said, "and I'm not used to this type of parking."

He shouted at me, "I don't care if you are from Kokomo, you can't drive like that in St. Maries!"

He looked at my driver's license and said, "Strobel, huh? You related to John at Rose Lake?"

"Yeah, my uncle. This is his pickup. I work for him." A familiar name seemed to be helping this situation.

Meanwhile, Jack was trying to peek out past Carl and me and said, "We, uh, parked our logging trucks over on the river road, heh, heh. We didn't want to park those big trucks here on Main Street. Too crowded here, you know. Heh, heh." He was gambling that the officer wouldn't go and check the trucks because it was out of the city limits. "We won't be riding very far like this."

The officer gave me back my driver's license but couldn't resist taking one more shot at me. "Damn it, Boy, if you ever drive like that again in St. Maries I'm going to write you up!"

There was only one answer for that. "Yes, sir," I replied.

We eased back to the trucks. Nobody followed us. It was starting to get light. This situation had had the potential to become very expensive, but we had escaped. No problems the rest of the way to camp.

That evening at dinner Jack waited until everybody was nearly done eating and then said loudly, "You guys want to hear a funny story? Well, let me tell you about

Clyde Peterson on left with Aunt Mildred.

the Kokomo Kid here," and pointed at me. My face was red as a beet as he related the morning events at St. Maries. With embellishments it was a fine story, all right. From then on most of the crew called me Kokomo Kid, but I didn't mind. I knew I had been accepted. No more homesickness for me.

Later that evening Clyde Peterson walked up to me and said, "I noticed you are pretty good with an ax."

"Well, thanks, I've chopped a lot of wood," I replied.

He went on, "I'm a sawyer and I hate chopping limbs. I'll make you a deal if you want to work with me. I'll fall the trees, you limb and tape measure for log length. I'll cut them up and scale them. Scaling is measuring to calculate how many board feet of lumber could be cut from a log. We get paid by how many thousand board feet we cut each day. If you have trouble with some of those brushy spruce trees, I'll help you limb. We'll go one third for you, one third for me and one third for the chainsaw. You have already cut enough firewood for a month, and John said it's okay with him if you want to work with me."

"I would like to give it a try," I told him. "It's a deal."

We shook hands, and he said, "Congratulations! You are now a gypo." A gypo is anybody who works in the woods and gets paid for how much he produces.

The power chain saws by the mid-1950s had become more dependable and were much lighter in weight than the first ones that showed up in the late 1940s. Up until that time trees were felled and cut into log lengths with a crosscut saw. This was a saw six or eight feet long that had large teeth with a handle at each end. Two men pulled it back and forth across the tree until it cut through. A very strenuous job, indeed!

The first power saws also required two men to operate them. The first problem was weight; they weighed one hundred pounds or more. One man controlled the motor and pushed a lever to make the chain holding the cutting teeth go around and around on a thin piece of grooved metal called the bar. A foot-long handle was fastened to the end of the bar, and another man held on to this to keep this unwieldy roaring monster on the tree and under control so they could make the cut. To carry one around in the brush on a steep hillside was exhausting enough, but these motors were so balky and hard to keep running that some loggers ran out of patience and cuss words and went back to their crosscut saws.

Clyde had a Homelite saw and it required daily tinkering. It ran fairly well and weighed about forty pounds. That was much too heavy to carry up the length of the felled tree to saw limbs off, so the limbs were cut off with an ax until the days of the lightweight saw arrived years later.

It wasn't long before I realized I had teamed up with one of the nicest men in the North Idaho woods. Before we started work the next morning he explained the safety rules for falling trees and pointed out the many ways to get hurt or, worse yet, killed. He talked about "widow-makers," standing dead trees with rot and deterioration that can fall at the slightest provocation: silent killer snags creating an instant widow.

Then there is the danger of a "barber chair." Most trees, when felled, break off the stump cleanly, falling well away from the sawyer; but sometimes the tree splits up the middle as it falls. At some point the underside of the tree breaks loose, leaving a long piece of wood (a slab) still attached to the stump. The result is that the rest of the tree shoots backward across the stump. If the sawyer doesn't get out of the way, it is almost certain death. Clyde had witnessed such an accident when he was young and shuddered as he talked about it.

I listened carefully, and memories of a tragic family accident came flooding back. In 1951 a freshly-cut log, unseen and unheard by my cousin Walter Strobel as he worked with a chain saw, rolled down the hill and killed him instantly. Clyde's instructions were accurate and appropriate and I started to realize this logging business was more dangerous than I thought.

The first trees to be cut on my first day on the job were tamarack. These tall, stately trees are the only trees in north Idaho with pinkish bark. The limbs are rather sparse for such big trees, and they chop off easily. Usually one whack was enough to separate the limb from the tree. It didn't take long to limb these trees at all.

I took the tape measure, stabbed the nail attached to the end of the tape into the big end of the fallen tree, walked out on the tree and made a notch with my ax at sixteen feet, four inches so that Clyde knew where to make the cut. I made another notch at thirty-two feet, eight inches, and so forth until I came to the top. My new caulk boots gripped the tree nicely. This work was just exhilarating. I whistled while I worked. This was the best job I had ever had!

Then Clyde cut down a nice, big spruce. The limbs came almost to the ground, looked to be about four inches apart and hung downward with no open spaces at all. I had never seen anything like it. "These spruce," Clyde advised, "you start at the top and work down."

He sawed up the last two tamaracks, sharpened the saw, gassed and oiled it up, and had a smoke. I was still lopping away on that spruce. Sweat trickled off my nose, and my shirt was sopping wet.

"Are there many more like this?" I gasped.

"Oh, yeah, here and there, now and then," he laughed.

By three o'clock quitting time, I had a knot on my chin from a mosquito bite, my feet hurt from the new shoes rubbing my toes, my knees and ankles were threatening to relocate to the same general area, and I checked to see if my knuckles were leaving drag marks in the dust.

Clyde was completely encouraging. "The first three days will be hard on you," he advised, "but after that you will get hardened into it. You will be fine. I like the way you handle that ax. You didn't cut off even one toe today."

Talk about being hungry! Now I understood why "the boys" roared out of the bunkhouses when the dinner bell rang.

Two truck drivers had moved into our bunkhouse, so we were full. Dick Moyer and O'Dell Hopper had both come from Oklahoma, "Okies" some people called them. They were really nice guys even though they talked funny. I didn't know anything about accents. "Oil" came out as "orl," and "tire" was "tar."

Clyde showed me how to build a fast fire in our stove. "Put in a little kindling, a block of wood, and splash some of this on it," he coached.

"Wait a minute. Is that gasoline?" I asked.

"Nope, diesel fuel." Gas would blow up, but diesel was okay, and the fire took off in a hurry. There was indeed a lot to learn. Just don't grab the wrong can.

Uncle John had a generator that supplied enough electricity to light the bunkhouses, a real luxury out in the woods. When he turned the generator off promptly at nine o'clock, it was wise to be in bed because it was usually pitch black. The nearest streetlight was twenty miles away.

The one type of light we did have was occasionally supplied by Mother Nature. One July night an electrical storm came up; it zeroed in on us. It was light as day with a pink hue when the lightning flashed and the thunder was deafening. I had never experienced anything like it. The next day we found three nearby trees had been hit by lightning.

Clyde and I settled into a nice routine. We worked well together. He was a good teacher and was patient with me. He convinced me I could do almost anything with my gloves on. Gloves off, gloves on was a waste of time. We took our gloves off to eat lunch, of course, and one day he noticed I was sitting on the bare ground.

"Never sit on the dirt like that. Sit on your gloves," he scolded. "You will get piles." I wasn't sure what piles were, but after a short discussion I knew he had given me good advice. He was forty-two years old, had worked in the woods all his life without a serious injury, and it wasn't all from good luck. He was careful.

I learned early on that he didn't always say what he meant. One day as he was cutting a tree down, he suddenly yelled, "Larry, get the hell out of here!" I was a bit startled, but ran up the hill. What he really meant to say was, "Larry, my young friend, I seem to be losing control of this tree, and since I don't have any idea where it is going to fall, it would be advantageous to your health and welfare if you would exit the general area immediately."

We got into an area that was mostly beetle-infested spruce. Hundreds of these trees were small, only six to ten inches at the stump, but were dying and had to go. They had lots of limbs, of course, but the worst part was the pitch that ran down the bark from top to bottom. It stuck to my boots, and every time I stepped in dirt, it stuck to the pitch, and pretty soon I was two inches taller. Clyde said, "You seem to be growing. Here, take this screwdriver and clean those boots before you slip and break a leg."

Uncle John came along to check on us, so we took a break and chatted. "See that big white pine log we cut this morning?" I asked Uncle John. It was about three feet across, and the center foot or so was pure rot. "What makes a tree rot like that?"

He rubbed his chin as if in deep thought, tipped his hat back on his head, took out a cigarette and lit it. Clyde and I relaxed and eagerly anticipated a learned dissertation from a long-time logger.

Finally he spoke. "Well, trees are like people. Some are sick and some ain't." With that he climbed into his pickup and drove quickly away.

Some days the trees fell with no problems. Other days a tree would hang up part way down, its limbs laced together with another tree. This was always a source of irritation for Clyde, and sometimes he could solve the problem by falling another tree across the offender. If that didn't work, we were in serious trouble. The whole mess could suddenly decide to fall—a very dangerous situation.

Clyde was easy-going, but hung-up trees made him mad. Then he would cut loose with some very innovative combinations of cuss words. One thing was consistent, though. He always started with "Dirty old…." After that you never knew. He made the kids from high school sound like amateurs. One afternoon he had three trees hang up, all crisscrossed, and he was so furious he quit a half hour early and went back to camp growling and muttering all the way.

Sometime after dinner he sneaked back over to see if anything had fallen. No such luck. This was about as dangerous a problem as he had ever created and a mistake could be fatal. He surveyed it from every angle, and later back at the bunkhouse he told me he thought he had the solution. "I'll fix those dirty old *#0&z*#x~*!!" he said.

Sure enough, the next morning he dropped one more and they all crashed down. I was way behind with my limbing right off the bat that day.

Clyde and I had felled and limbed about a hundred trees in a large meadow (swamp is a more accurate word) and left them in tree lengths. These would have to be dragged out to solid ground with the bulldozer—no road could be built there.

The day came to start pulling out these large spruce trees. I was to be the choker setter. A choker is an eight-foot length of one-inch cable with a metal hook attached to one end and an adjustable fitting called a bell at the other. Encircle the tree at the big end and cinch up the bell fitting. The harder it's pulled, the tighter it "chokes" and will not slip off the tree. Attach the hook at the other end of the choker to the hook on the long cable reeled out from a spool (drum) on the dozer and the tree is reeled in like a giant lazy fish. Then the tree is skidded to a landing where a sawyer (Clyde in this case) cuts it into log lengths ready to be loaded on a truck.

The bulldozer operator was a fiftyish fellow named Keith "Slim" Dowell. Hardly anyone knew his real name. He was always referred to as "Slim." Probably the only people who referred to him as Keith were the electric power company and the Internal Revenue Service.

Slim was a big man, about six feet, three inches, and not at all slim any more. He had big, beefy hands and big feet with shoes scuffed beyond hope. His face was broad with a large nose. His voice was loud and gravelly. He wore an ancient Stetson hat with a hole in the crown, and it looked as if it needed an oil change. His black shirt and black pants always appeared to be rumpled. What didn't show until I got to know him better was the fact that under that rumpled shirt beat a heart of pure gold.

Slim was a smoker, of course. Every other smoker in camp took his pack of cigarettes out of his shirt pocket, shook one out, tapped it on his thumb nail two or three times, ripped a match out of a matchbook, lit up and started sucking tar into his lungs. Elapsed time was under one minute. Slim, for what reason I never knew, insisted on rolling his own. First, he slithered a little packet of cigarette papers out of his pocket and licked his index finger to try to get a single paper separated from the others. After several attempts, one came loose, but it was already quite damp. He pulled the tobacco pouch from another pocket. Now it got tricky. His face took on a look of deep concentration as he tried to pour tobacco out of the pouch onto this little bitty piece of white paper. His large fingers weren't very agile any more, but he got an "A" for effort as tobacco spilled past the paper. Finally, he'd have a satisfactory amount on the paper and fumbled the pouch back into his pocket after pulling the drawstring tight with his teeth. Now to level the tobacco out evenly on the paper was

Slim Dowell, center, with two hunting partners ca. 1945. Photo courtesy of Helen Strobel Chatfield.

a losing proposition, so after a feeble attempt at that, he licked the sticky edge of the paper to seal this masterpiece together. He always seemed to get way too much saliva involved at this point, so the end result was a cigarette small on each end, very fat in the middle and so soggy a blow torch would be challenged to light it. That didn't phase Slim any. He fished around in another pocket for a wooden match and then had to find a place to strike it. If all else failed, he would strike it on the back of his pant leg in a fast swooping motion. The friction would light the match all right and leave a little puff of smoke drifting away from the vicinity of his right hip. Then he had the problem of getting the soggy thing lit. Usually after two or three attempts, he actually got it going. After he took a drag or two, the darn thing would go out. Since he was expected to get some work done that day, he would drive around on the dozer for an hour with this soggy, misshapen, unlit cigarette clamped between his lips. At least he wasn't pouring tar into his lungs, but I worried about the danger of lip cancer. One hour and seventeen wooden matches later he would flip his cigarette butt over the side of the dozer and calculate when he would have time to roll another smoke.

I was getting two dollars per hour to flounder around in that swamp setting chokers and dragging cable. This was considered a generous wage in those days. I didn't know what Clyde and his saw were getting up at the landing, but he had the better deal. After board and taxes were taken out I cleared less than $10 for a day.

This job wasn't too bad except for the mosquitoes. There were swarms of them. Slim was sympathetic and sprayed me all over with bug repellant, which was semi-effective. While he was gone with a load to the landing, I would hurry to set the chokers and then run up to an open sunny place Slim had pointed out. The mosquitoes didn't like it there because it was too hot.

At lunchtime Slim and Clyde and I sat on some logs at the landing to get away from those pesky mosquitoes. It came to Slim that he needed to blow his nose. He held his coffee cup in his right hand and a sandwich in his left hand. Everyone I had previously known would, in this situation, set both objects down and yank a handkerchief out of his pocket. Slim must not have believed in setting food around where an ant might walk across it or something. He held the base of his right thumb against his nose and blew. He got fairly good results and didn't spill any coffee. Then he dragged his left shirtsleeve across his nose and wiped his shirtsleeve on his left pant leg. This he accomplished without violating his sandwich in any way whatsoever. He was basically a kind and considerate man who wouldn't have purposely offended anyone with his table manners. He must have wondered what I was snickering about. Hoo Boy! My education was in full gallop.

That evening as we sat in the cook shack eating dinner, Slim waited until it was quiet except for the sounds of eating and then said loudly enough for everybody to hear, "Those mosquitoes were sure terrible down there in that swamp today." I heard one "uh, huh" from somewhere, but everybody ignored the remark and kept chewing. After a short pause, "I sure felt sorry for Larry fighting those swarms all day. A tough job he had."

A couple of "Uh huhs," a "Yup," and an "Mmmm" were the only responses.

I knew this master prankster was setting up the whole crew and wondered how he would finish them off. A longer pause, and then here it came.

"I tell you, them ain't the biggest mosquitoes I've ever seen, but they sure as hell are different."

That one hung in the air like a suspended water balloon. The clock on the wall seemed to stop ticking. Stella looked like a statue holding a gravy ladle as she stared at Slim. A hardworking fellow named George sat across the table from me. He stopped chewing and looked up. He couldn't stand it any longer. "How, uh, how ARE they different, Slim?" BINGO!!

Now Slim shifted into his most authoritative voice. "Well, if you turn them over on their backs, you will notice they have a white spot on their bellies about the size of a fifty-cent piece," and he finished the sentence with a little snort through his nose that he always gave after making a profound statement. The cook shack shook with laughter, and George cursed himself for being the one to take the bait. I knew I needed to remember how Slim had done this. This was education I might need.

The next afternoon we had nearly finished the "swamp job" when we heard shouting from across a small canyon. My cousin Jack was motioning and yelling that he needed the bulldozer to come over right away. I went with Slim, and we went clanking and clattering along the road around the end of the canyon.

We soon saw the problem. Jack had driven the loading crane in on a short dead-end road where several large piles of logs were stacked. The road seemed a little soft, but not too bad. One of the truck drivers backed in, unloaded the trailer and was prepared to be loaded. It looked like another routine load of logs coming up. Two men called hookers each set a hook, often called a dog, in both ends of the log, and it was

Jack Strobel loading logs with the Michigan loading crane. Bill Jacquemin and Dick Donahoe are the hookers.

lifted via a cable up and onto the truck by the crane. As they piled logs on the truck, it seemed to settle a little. More logs, and the tires started disappearing into the mud. Jack, the hookers, and truck driver stared as it sank faster and faster. It stopped when the bunks, the ten-foot wide iron bars that the logs sat on, hit the ground.

What a sight! A load of logs enclosed in four stakes, stuck in a mud hole with a truck cab looking up at the trees!

Jack and the hookers started unloading the truck while the driver ran off in search of John. He found him about a quarter of a mile up the road sitting in his pickup adding columns of numbers in his notebook.

Breathlessly the driver related the chain of events leading up to Mother Earth almost swallowing one of his trucks. Uncle John was one of the coolest, calmest, most unshakable men I've ever known.

"The hell you say!" he responded.

He was so in control that if somebody had come running up to him and shouted that nearby Round Top Mountain blew its stack and molten lava was running into the Clearwater River, he would have no doubt said, "The hell you say!"

This comment bought him a little time to then go into deep thought in search of a solution to the problem at hand. For this situation the enormous power of his bulldozer was the answer.

By pulling with the bulldozer and lifting with the crane, they got the truck to solid ground. Now the crane was trapped by this giant mud hole. Jack piled logs into the mud hole until he could drive the crane over them and escape.

This was typical of the surprises involved with logging. The ground finally dried enough to load these logs, but they were the last to go at the end of the summer.

Most of the loggers in camp were family men trying to make a living and get along. They disliked being away from their families during the week, but accepted it as a way of life. They were mostly a sober bunch; a beer here and there on the weekend was the extent of their drinking. However, there is always an exception.

Skidding jammer set up to pull logs up the hill to be decked. Photo courtesy of Lawrence Hoiland.

Ben Hunter, Bobby Arkslander, and Harry Healey made up one of the jammer crews that skidded and decked the logs. A jammer was a homemade piece of machinery invented and built, I do believe, by some ingenious engineer posing as a wintertime unemployed logger. Jim Casey is given credit by some for building the first jammer. No machinery company in the United States ever built one to my knowledge, and they were unique to north Idaho. Why was this piece of equipment called a jammer? I don't know. Why was a jammer operator called a "jammer puncher"? I don't know that either. It is logger slang comparable to a bulldozer operator being called a "cat skinner".

To build one of these machines required a large truck. First of all, a large powerful engine was mounted sideways behind the truck cab. Then a platform was built on the frame. Two fifteen-foot spar poles, usually in the shape of an "A," were mounted straight up in metal fittings over the dual-wheeled rear axle. Another log called a boom, about 30 to 40 feet long, was attached to a metal fitting at a forty-five degree angle out over the back of the truck and fitted at the top end with a metal cap with an attached pulley. There were many variations on how to rig a jammer, but all were similar. It took a man with welding skills and a thorough knowledge of power take-off gears, chains, pulleys, and belts all winter to build one.

The jammer setup was accomplished with cable threaded through three block and tackle hooked to stumps or trees to create a rectangle, with the jammer being the fourth corner of said rectangle. Two large spools of cable were used; cable from spool #1, called the "main line", was hand-pulled down the road about 100 feet, run through the pulley on the first block and tackle, pulled downhill for 200 to 300 hundred feet, through the second block and tackle, and across the hill to the third block and tackle directly below the jammer. Cable from spool #2 was pulled downhill and connected to cable #1 with metal rings that held the tongs. Run spool #1 forward and the tongs pulled a log uphill. Run spool #2 forward and the empty tongs were pulled back down the hill; this was called the "haul back".

A power take-off from the motor mounted on the truck ran the whole thing. There was always a magnificent array of wheels and belts, chains and gears, working in unison. It required two feet and two arms and good coordination to run the clutch, brake, and cable controls.

The crew required three men. The jammer puncher sat on a seat and pulled logs uphill after the hooker downhill hooked tongs onto the end of a log. The "hooker" blew a police whistle with a prearranged number of toots for stop, go, or wait, the tongs pulled loose, or whatever. The deck man unhooked the tongs if needed, chopped off any limbs still attached to the log, wrote the log length with crayon on the end of each log, and sometimes hit the log end with a branding hammer to identify which company owned the log. All logs were piled neatly in decks beside the road to be loaded onto trucks. The deck was always piled against a standing tree or two or against stumps so the logs wouldn't roll back down the hill. If you heard a story about a jammer puncher who was so good at decking logs that he piled them successfully against huckleberry bushes, you knew you were visiting with that great storyteller, Slim Dowell.

Cables from the A-frame and boom attached to trees or stumps above the road

Jammer built by Carl Hoiland. Photo courtesy of Carl Hoiland.

anchored the jammer. There was a lot of sheer power and force involved as the hooked log plowed through brush and windfalls and bounced off stumps. The jammer shook and rattled and bounced. The cable sang as it zipped through the pulleys. A well-tuned engine and a well-trained and coordinated crew could deck a lot of logs in a day; the steeper the hill, the better. The idea was to lift the log off the ground as soon as possible on the journey up the hill. This was the reason for the long boom. The skidding process was always uphill; it was a good method and kept erosion to a minimum. After the logs from a "strip" were all decked, everything was unhooked, the jammer was moved up the road a ways and then set up, tied down, and cable strung again. A good crew could move in thirty to forty minutes. Jammer crews loved steep hills and sawyers hated them.

Ben, Bobby, and Harry were close friends, had worked together for years and were very good at their jobs. When they felt good and the weather was nice, they meshed together like the inside workings of a clock.

We usually worked from 6 to 10 am on Saturday, loaded up our dirty clothes and headed for home. Then we drove back Sunday evening, allowing time to arrive and be in bed by nine o'clock when the lights went out. The men all did well with this schedule except for the aforementioned jammer crew.

These three always started back to camp on time, but would find themselves needing something to quench their thirst before they got into the woods. Without fail, stopping for a beer soon turned into serious drinking, and by Sunday evening at nine o'clock they could be just about anywhere between home and camp.

Their normal arrival time was always somewhere between 9 pm Sunday and 9 am Monday. The most likely time of arrival was midnight to 3 am when they came roaring into the parking lot. They would spill out of the car yelling, laughing,

Skidding jammer at work in winter. Photo courtesy of Lawrence Hoiland.

and shoving, slamming the doors numerous times, bumping into things in the dark, dropping things, falling down, helping each other up, maybe singing a song or two, and that was before they got to their bunkhouse.

This was a most unwelcome interruption to the sleep of everybody else, but there is something entertaining about a group of happy drunks, and after a few curses everybody was sound asleep again. Most of the crew just accepted them as they were and didn't hassle them too much. Besides, what can you say to a man who looks deathly ill when he awakes?

It was a foregone conclusion that these three would not work on Monday. I asked Uncle John why he put up with them. "They can skid as many logs in four days as most crews can in five," he answered. "Jammer crews are hard to find. What would you do?"

"Point well taken," I said.

The usual Monday morning found the three happy partiers too sick to even consider breakfast, but, to our astonishment, one bright and sunny Monday morning here came Harry. He had on his work pants and a tee shirt riddled with holes. He hadn't pulled up his suspenders, and they flopped at his sides as he shuffled along. His work boots were beyond his ability at the moment so he had on a pair of brown leather slippers with the elastic sides that ninety-nine percent of North Idaho loggers wore. Beads of sweat covered his forehead, and his face was the color of a fire engine. His hair was sticking seven different directions, and he needed a shave. His eyes were about half open, and what was visible looked like a road map of Tennessee.

He plopped down on the bench, and as the food was passed, he would look at it, hesitate, and pass it on. He just couldn't force himself to fork anything onto his plate. Everybody else was eating a hearty breakfast, and his plate looked like Mother Hubbard's cupboard. He looked around and spotted a bowl of peaches down the table. Harry had a speech impediment that prevented him from pronouncing L's and R's.

He stared wearily at the peaches and said, "Pees pass the fute." He helped himself to two pieces of peach and a little bit of syrup. He managed two bites and a taste of syrup. By now sweat was pouring down his face. "Scuse me," he mumbled and got unsteadily to his feet. He staggered to the door, leaned on the door jam, and stared at the bunkhouse. It must have looked to be a mile away.

Clyde looked at me, smiled, shook his head, and said, "How can he never learn? How can three such good workers, all really good guys, never learn? I quit having that kind of fun many years ago." So my education was coming along. You never know what you might learn at breakfast.

There were two other sawyers in camp; brothers Tom and Mike Jacobson were career woods workers and darned good at their jobs. Uncle John insisted Clyde and I work at least one-half mile from them to eliminate the possibility of a falling tree hitting another sawyer.

These two lived in Coeur d'Alene and preferred to spend Sunday evening with their families. They also didn't like to have their sleep interrupted by noisy happy drunks so they always started back to camp about 3 am, arriving in time for breakfast at 5:30 am. Mike was quite a storyteller and once told me with a straight face, "Oh yeah, we had our first baby nine months and five minutes after our wedding."

Jammers were often used to load trucks. Museum of North Idaho photo.

One night after dinner I heard more clamor than normal from one of the bunkhouses. I moseyed up to see what was happening. As with many evenings, a poker game was in progress, and this was a boisterous one. Some of the boys had rolled an old empty wooden cable spool in, laid it on its side and covered it with a blanket. Blocks of wood were good enough for chairs. Silver dollars clanked onto the table and changed hands rapidly. It was exciting but intimidating. I had played a little bit with my high school friends, but after watching for a while realized this game was way beyond my area of expertise. I wasn't making enough money to chance losing it to these friendly sharks. They were nice guys, but they played for keeps.

These poker games were why my cousin Wilbur (everybody called him Willy) wasn't in camp this year. The previous summer had seen Willy go through a bad, bad streak of cards. Cousin Jack had bought new bikes for his kids with his winnings, and Willy wished he had bikes to sell. His wife Jeri had been furious, so to prevent their budget from being devastated again Willy was working close to home this summer.

Willy was thirty-one now. He was only about my height but was wide-bodied and tended to be pudgy. He had the first stages of Dunlop's Disease (his stomach done lopped over his belt). He had large, dreamy-looking brown eyes (some of the ladies referred to them as "bedroom eyes)", a radiant smile, a charming manner and a friendly line of gab. It was next to impossible to dislike him. He loved to play poker but, due to his optimistic nature, was prone to chase cards on impossible hands.

This game called poker had gotten him into trouble before. After high school Uncle John decided Willy should go to college. At the appropriate time Uncle John and Willy went to the University of Idaho at Moscow, got him enrolled and settled into a dormitory. After making a few calculations, Uncle John opened a checking account at a nearby bank. As he gave Willy the checkbook he said, "There is enough money here to easily see you through the school year. I expect you to apply yourself, study and get decent grades."

Uncle John drove home feeling good. He was secure in the knowledge he had done the right thing that day.

It was seven weeks later Willy showed up at Rose Lake on a Sunday morning. Uncle John was sitting at the kitchen table relaxing with a cup of coffee and the Sunday paper. He had not a care in the world when he noticed Willy peeking in the back door.

"Well! Hi, Willy! What brings you home?" asked Uncle John.

"Well…I, uh," was as far as Willy got.

"All your clothes are dirty, I suppose," teased Uncle John. John loved to tease his children.

"Uh, yeah. I mean, no, uh… Gee!"

"Well, then, what is it?" asked John.

"Well, I, uh, see, had a little bad luck," stammered Willy.

"Like what?" Uncle John didn't like the sound of this.

"Well, there was this little poker game in the dorm sometimes, see, and my cards weren't too good, and I lost some, and then I had to play more to catch up, but I didn't. The truth is I'm broke."

"The hell, you say!"

Uncle John leaned back in his chair, clasped his hands behind his head, stared at the ceiling and retreated into deep thought. Willy stood on one foot and then the other as the clock ticked loudly. After several minutes the front legs of the chair hit the floor with a thud.

"Willy," John said, "Get in your car, go back to Moscow, pack up and come home. Your college career is over. You'll start working for me tomorrow morning."

Willy had always been a fun-loving and carefree spirit. As a boy he had a habit of sneaking out at night. Uncle John and Aunt Mildred had done their best to keep him under control, but lovable as he was, he had been a hard case.

Several years back Willy had set a family record of sorts. Due to a very confusing mix-up concerning incoming and outgoing wives, he had become a father after only six weeks of marriage to Jeri. His friends razzed him about being the fastest gun in the West and called him Speedy Strobel, but, as usual, he was good-natured about it all.

It was a rare day, indeed, that Willy became upset or lost that engaging, ever-present smile, but he had run afoul of that prankster Slim Dowell last summer. Slim loved to fish, and one Friday evening he decided to go fishing in some creeks near the camp instead of going home for the weekend. If he did any good he would donate the fish for a camp dinner.

Since he was twenty miles from a phone, he had to somehow let his wife Eileen know he wouldn't be coming home. A group of the boys were lounging around their bunkhouse after dinner. Slim was busy rolling a smoke. He had just gotten the tobacco arranged on that little white paper when he erupted with a loud sneeze. The tobacco flew off the paper and splattered on the floor. For Slim it was just part of the game; he hardly growled as he got out his tobacco pouch again.

Then he had an idea. "Hey Willy," he called over, "You will be going right by my place when you go home tomorrow afternoon. How about stopping to tell Eileen I am staying up here to fish all weekend? I don't want her worrying."

"Oh, sure, fine. I can do that," was the reply.

Slim finished rolling his latest creation and held it up for a long look. He had to decide which end to put in his mouth and which end to light.

"Hey Willy," Slim yelled, "Tell Eileen you came by to take care of my homework for me." He gave that little snort.

The bunkhouse erupted in laughter. Anybody who knew the Dowells recognized this remark as a real knee-slapper. To be unfaithful was not in either's makeup.

Willy loved a prank as much as anybody, and on the drive home he got to thinking about what Slim had said. This had real potential, he decided.

As he parked in front of the Dowell home he had second thoughts. What if she was embarrassed and he felt really bad? "Naw," he thought, "This is too good to pass up." He walked to the door, relishing the upcoming conversation. He knocked on the door and waited. The order of conversation went like this:

Willy: (Big grin on his face) "Hiya, Eileen."

Eileen: (Smiling pleasantly) "Well, hi, Willy. What brings you by?"

Willy: (Bigger grin now) "Slim wanted me to drop by and tell you he is staying in camp this weekend to go fishing."

Eileen (Pleasant smile continuing) "Oh, he is? Well, okay. I sure do appreciate you coming by to tell me."

Willy: (Biggest grin possible) "Yeah, he told me to come by and tell you I'm supposed to take care of his homework."

Eileen: (Smile gone, neck arched, eyes snapping) "WHAT?"

Willy: (Grin fading fast)

Eileen: "WHAT?"

Willy: (Grin gone completely)

Eileen: "What in the HELL is the matter with him? Sending a BOY down here when there's MAN'S work to be done!" She stepped back and slammed the door.

Willy felt like he was standing on an exploding box of dynamite. Here he'd been pole-axed by a woman. "Damn it, anyway," he muttered as he went slinking back to his car. "How did I let that get out of control so fast?" He'd forgotten that she had lived with Mr. Prankster for years and learned how to fight back, that's how.

When Slim found out on Monday what had happened he became nearly hysterical with laughter. This little prank had far outdistanced his wildest dreams. He couldn't wait to get home and congratulate Eileen. "By golly!" he thought, "We'll get all gussied up and go down to Coeur d'Alene for dinner to celebrate."

A camp cook didn't have an easy job. Stella arose by three o'clock each morning and built a fire in the big cook stove to get underway with the day's cooking and baking. She worked by lantern light. The refrigerator was a group of wooden boxes arranged in the creek. The water was cold enough to prevent spoilage. By five-thirty she was always ready.

Sometimes in the evening she would call across the yard and motion me over. She would ask me to dispose of several five-gallon buckets of garbage. I would lug them down the creek to a soft, swampy area and dig a hole; we had to bury it because of the bears.

When I returned there would be a big piece of pie on the table. She would say, "I just happened to have some extra pie. I've got to figure a way to get some meat onto those bones of yours."

We would sit and visit, and one night she asked if I liked working in the woods.

"Oh, yeah," I replied.

She thought awhile and then said, "You might work in the woods some, but you'll never be a lumberjack. You've been schooled as a musician. You should do something with that. Not many people can."

Later that week one of the truck drivers quit and I said to Uncle John, "Instead of hiring another driver, why don't you teach me to drive?"

He was slow to answer. "Because if I do, you'll end up working in the woods the rest of your life, and I don't think that's right for you. No, I'm not going to do it."

I was disappointed, but I had a lot of respect for him and said no more about it. I knew I needed to trust his judgment.

Uncle John was fifty-four, well known for his love of food, and had developed a good bit of a paunch. To be polite, he looked prosperous. It hadn't always been this way. He had been raised in an area that didn't have a school. Finally he went to school for two years where he learned basic reading, writing and arithmetic. At age fourteen he went to work in the woods.

Years later, Uncle John started his logging company with one little truck. He realized there was opportunity to make money logging so he borrowed forty thousand dollars to buy equipment. It took him ten years to pay that loan off. By then he had learned the hard lessons he needed to know and was on his way to success. He was shrewd and clever and had made big money logging in areas others thought impossible. To pay off that kind of debt in the 1930s and 40s was a remarkable feat.

Theirs was a hardworking, close-knit family. Wife Mildred, besides being mother to five children, kept all the books and cooked in the logging camps. Daughter Helen, starting at age fourteen, learned her cooking skills in the camps. The three boys learned to run equipment at an early age. Jack started driving logging truck when he was twelve. Things were a little easier by the time Betty came along, but there was always plenty of work to be done. There had been some lean years, but they always kept going.

Uncle John had driven the bulldozer himself for years, but when he could afford it had hired Slim Dowell. John and Slim were close friends, but a stranger listening to them would never have known that. They repeatedly told stories on each other. The slightest slip-up could be ballooned into a major event. I had never realized that exaggeration could be turned into an art form.

Uncle John still drove the dozer sometimes on the weekend, if there was a need to get a road built in a hurry.

One evening we were all sitting around enjoying the beautiful weather, and Slim, master of exaggerated detail, launched into a great story. According to Slim, John called him one Sunday evening and casually said, "Slim, I left the dozer up on that new timber sale back of Killarney Lake. I got the road built up to the top of that big ridge. Go on down the other side of the ridge. You will see the blaze marks on the trees where I want the road to go."

When Slim got there the next morning, he claimed the dozer was balanced on a pinnacle of rock with 95% of the tracks hanging in midair.

"I don't know how he climbed off without it rolling right off the mountain," Slim said.

Slim studied the situation so long he had time to roll a smoke and fire it up. When he finally got up nerve enough to step up on the dozer it swayed and rocked back and forth, and it took the skill of a genius to move it to safety. He was so relieved he seriously considered going to church the next Sunday, he declared.

John countered with a story of Slim sliding off a new road, with the dozer completely out of control, ending up in a creek bottom stuck among boulders with windfalls crisscrossed all around. John claimed Slim spent all day building a mile of useless road just to get the dozer back to where it belonged in the first place. Besides all that, Slim was costing him a lot of money, and he didn't know why he kept an inept operator around anyway.

Slim roared right back claiming John was so absent-minded that one morning on his way to a job site at the head of Killarney Lake, he suddenly realized he was approaching the Blue Lagoon Tavern—a full mile past the Killarney lake turnoff. He turned around, went back, and turned off all right, but was so forgetful that he forgot

John Strobel cooling off on a hot day.

the spring flood was underway. The lower road was flooded, but John didn't notice, drove right out into the water and finally got the hint when his feet got all wet.

"If it weren't for competent, hardworking employees like me," said Slim, "he would've been in bankruptcy court years ago." This was such a profound revelation that Slim ended with a double snort.

At this point I thought Uncle John was getting beaten pretty badly in this little discussion. How could he recover from a shot like that?

John pushed his battered Stetson hat back on his head and said, "Is that so? Well, Slim, let's talk about the day you drove twenty miles up into the woods, decided to gas up the dozer and discovered you had an empty fifty-gallon barrel in the back of your pickup. Considering you had to drive all the way back to Rose Lake, fill the barrel and go back to the job, how much money you suppose you made me that day? Where was your mind like a steel trap that day?"

Slim blinked about six times and said, "Dammit, John, I had completely forgotten about that. Why haven't you? But what about the time..."

Around and around they went, the stories getting bigger and better, more involved, with the exaggerations completely out of control.

When this session ended, I thought Slim was ahead by about three points. It had been a great game.

The month of August arrived, and the weather got hot. Back in Rose Lake, Aunt Mildred noticed that the lawn had grown quickly and really needed to be mowed. Uncle John always took care of it on his short weekend and he bought an electric

Rose Lake, Idaho, a busy, prosperous lumber town in 1911. Museum of North Idaho photo.

mower because it was fast. No more having to keep a can of gas in the garage, no more tinkering with a balky engine when he was pressed for time—just plug in the cord and zip around the yard.

Mildred decided to do John a big favor because she knew he would be tired from the heat. She called Jack, a teenaged boy who lived down the road, and hired him to mow the lawn.

"John will be real happy he doesn't have to do that," she thought.

Young Jack arrived and she helped him get the mower out of the garage and on his way. The whir of the motor passed the kitchen window and she was congratulating herself on the ease of getting the grass taken care of. Then she didn't hear the whir anymore. Before she could investigate, there was a knock at the back door.

"Mrs. Strobel," said Jack sheepishly, "I ran over the cord and cut it in two."

Mildred sighed and kept her composure. She would just call the town handyman to come over and splice the cord. Luckily he was home. She and Jack sat in the shade and waited. "It sure is quiet," she told Jack. "It's nothing like the good old days when the sawmill was still here. It used to be a hustle, bustle place with trucks and people going in all directions."

Indeed, Rose Lake had been a rip-snorting place with schools, churches and businesses, plus lots of houses and a tavern or two. Then the sawmill burned and, like so many lumber towns, the mill owners took a hard look at the remaining close-by timber and decided it was not economically feasible to rebuild.

Rose Lake Lumber Co. ca. 1920. The town declined quickly after the mill closed in 1928. Museum of North Idaho photo.

Now the town was so quiet that old Rover could flop down in the dust in the middle of King Street, take an afternoon nap, and never be threatened by any harm. Even the flies and mosquitoes took the afternoon off.

The birds and beavers and muskrats across the highway from the Strobel house in Porter Lake were completely quiet, too. It was more of a brushy swamp than lake and Uncle John said it was worthless. "Too thick to drink and too thin to plow," was his description. In later years it would be called "a valuable wildlife sanctuary."

Within an hour the cord was spliced and the mower was whirring again. Jack got back to work, and Mildred went back into the house.

About three minutes later the whir stopped: Another knock at the back door.

"Mrs. Strobel, I cut the cord again," Jack confessed.

This was way beyond her tolerance level. She flipped Jack a fifty-cent piece and barked. "Put the mower in the garage and get the hell out of here!"

She slammed the door as she went stomping into the kitchen. She was fuming mad, but before she could collect her thoughts there was another knock at the back door. It was Jack again.

"Mrs. Strobel, the mower handle slipped out of my hand and went right through the window."

"What's the use?" she said, as she threw her hands into the air. She started to laugh. Tears ran down her cheeks as she laughed harder and harder. Her intentions had been so good. She would have to explain to John that she had tried, and she hoped he wouldn't be too tired to splice the cord, mow the lawn and replace a window.

One August afternoon it was close to quitting time, and I waited while Clyde sawed up the last tree. "Let's fall that great big spruce," he said. "We won't have to mess with it the first thing in the morning."

This giant was about three feet through, but tapered fast for about six feet. He made the under cut, and this looked like another routine falling job. When he had sawed in quite a way, he yanked the saw out and motioned. I stepped up and jammed two wedges into the cut and gave them several whacks with our sledgehammer. The spruce creaked as it slowly started to ease over. I grabbed the wedges and stepped back.

I was watching the upper limbs and saw a limb break off an adjoining tree and fly back towards us. No big deal. I would just sidestep it. I was aware that Clyde was yelling, "Run! Run! RUN!" I didn't. The falling limb landed with no harm. Then I glanced down at the stump and saw what he had been yelling about. The tree split up the middle as it fell, the much feared problem called a "barber chair". Inexplicably the bottom five feet shattered, but had not broken loose and shot the tree back across the stump. The tree was still attached to the stump by shards of splintered wood.

I looked at Clyde. His face was the color of chalk and he looked to be on the verge of tears as he fumbled for his cigarettes. His hands shook when he lit up.

"If those few splinters hadn't held, that whole tree would have shot back over the stump, and you would have been driven into the ground like a tack," he said.

By all rights I should have been lying squashed under the butt of that tree, and here I stood. It suddenly hit me hard. I had stood on the doorstep of death and hadn't been touched. An obituary flashed through my mind—Mine.

"Let's go," Clyde said, "I don't feel like working any more today."

Back at camp we both lay on our beds thinking. We said very little. I had almost become a woods statistic. There must be a good reason I had been spared, and life was taking on a new meaning. The typical teenager seems to think he is immortal. Maybe this was more education than I had bargained for.

John's truck drivers hauled the logs through Avery to a railroad siding upriver away from the congestion of town. A loading crane parked there lifted the logs off the trucks and set them onto railroad flat cars. John kept a crew of three in Avery to handle this job. They stayed at the hotel. We rarely saw this Avery crew, but they occasionally came up for an evening of poker. They were noisy, rude, and crude and I could only imagine a typical evening with them in an Avery tavern.

The logs went by rail to a siding called Ramsey on the lower part of the St. Joe River, where they were dumped into the water and towed to the Russell and Pugh sawmill at Springston. This was a little town on the Coeur d'Alene River about one mile upstream from the lakeshore town of Harrison.

It was a fact; there really wasn't any law in Avery. If the sheriff at Wallace got wind of a murder, he would mosey on over at his earliest convenience, but other than that, law enforcement just ignored the place. It was too remote to worry about.

Avery did have women, though, at least at the end of the week. It occurred to me, as the summer went along, that there is a direct correlation between a man's glands and his eyesight. All the truck drivers were married men and went home for

Springston, Idaho. The logs Clyde and Larry sawed ended up at the Russell and Pugh Mill in Springston. Museum of North Idaho photo.

the weekend. They had ample time to look around as they drove through Avery. The week went like this:

Monday: There must have been no women in sight. At the evening gabfest none of them mentioned seeing a female.

Tuesday: Somebody would mention seeing one or two homely, overweight women in town.

Wednesday: "Say, I saw some pretty darn nice-looking women in Avery today."

Thursday: "Oh, yeah! You should have seen the well-built, really good-looking women strolling around in Avery today."

Friday: "Whoooeee! I'll tell you what! The women in Avery are just---Well, I swear there aren't any prettier women anywhere on the face of this earth."

Strange how the population of a little town can change like that. Every week, too.

One day in mid-August my parents, Earl and Beulah, decided to drive up and see this camp I had been telling them about. I had warned them about strictly following the "stay left" and "stay right" signs on the Fishhook Creek Road.

Even though the sign said "stay left," Dad wasn't comfortable doing that. Sure enough, not long after they crossed over to the left, here came a loaded Euclid. My mother screamed and covered her eyes. Dad slammed on the brakes and held the steering wheel in a death grip. The Euclid passed on their right with a whoosh.

The first one is always the worst, and they negotiated the rest of the miles to camp with a minimum of difficulty. The scenery was spectacular, and they enjoyed seeing an unfamiliar area.

They were waiting when Clyde and I came in from work. I felt proud as I introduced Clyde and referred to him as my partner. Nobody had any trouble figuring out who my dad was. He looked like a smaller edition of John.

Dick Donahoe came along and met them. "Nice to meet the parents of the Kokomo Kid," he said.

"What's that?" my dad asked.

"Who?" from my mother.

I had neglected to tell them the details of the St. Maries adventure.

Dick, a high-spirited rascal, was married to my cousin Betty. He loved to tell stories and apparently had been understudying Slim Dowell for years.

Dick fired up his version of the Kokomo Kid story, and since he was well-schooled in the art of exaggeration, it came out sounding like I was some sort of folk hero. Dad thought it was hilarious. Mom never really understood these things and was more perplexed than regaled.

They met Stella. My mother couldn't imagine how one woman could put out that much food for one meal. They stayed for supper in the cook shack and sat together with me and John's boys.

"Taste this gravy, Mom," I said. "Isn't it just great? We have gravy every night."

I didn't belittle my mother's cooking, but I sure praised Stella's. Mom had never been big on making gravy, and sometimes when she did, she made a concoction she called "egg gravy." I hated it, and though I didn't have the nerve to tell her, it was awful. We had lots more good gravy at home after that visit, and after observing and talking to Stella she tried harder and made some great meals.

It was getting well along in August, and the day came when Clyde fell the last tree of the timber sale. He and I were done at the camp.

As I was saying my goodbyes, Dick Moyer took me aside.

"I know you've had a good summer here," he said with his Oklahoma accent. "Take my advice and find another line of work. The mud, the mosquitoes, the breakdowns, the constant danger—it isn't worth it." He was completely sincere. I had thought the woods would be my life's work, but the seeds of doubt had been planted by too many people.

Before I left I told Uncle John, "I think I'll enroll at North Idaho Junior College this fall."

"The hell, you say!" was his predictable response. He told me the reasons why my decision was a good one. He was obviously pleased.

Clyde and I worked together for two more weeks cutting trees in the mountains west of Killarney Lake. We drove out from home each morning; it was okay, but it wasn't like camp life.

One morning as we approached the work area, Clyde lit a cigarette and noticed he had only three left in the pack. "Grab me a pack of cigarettes out of the glove compartment," he said. I looked in—no cigarettes.

"I think there's a carton in the back seat," he said. I leaned over the seat and couldn't find any there either. We parked at the job site.

"Well, I'm sure there are some in the trunk," he said with sincere confidence.

The trunk couldn't produce any cigarettes either. Three cigarettes and we are nine hours away from getting home. He looked panic stricken.

"Dirty old…" He started talking really fast, going into a tirade of exploding expletives.

"I don't need cigarettes anyway! I can go without them! I should quit anyway! It's a dirty habit! I should never have started! Don't you ever start!"

His fury spent, the fact was he did need them. He quietly sat down on a stump, measured the length of a cigarette, and then arithmetically concluded how far he could smoke each cigarette if he lit up every half hour. So for the rest of the day he would light up, puff really fast through the allotted inch or so, put it out and back into the pack. Good thing he had lots of matches.

We were cutting an area burned over in a forest fire many years before, leaving the strong and durable tamarack trees that could survive a fast-moving fire. They had become rotten, unstable and extremely dangerous to fall. Clyde made me stay way back; touch the saw to them and look out! One fell over while he was making the undercut, another collapsed downward onto the stump before it fell. Clyde was cursing and running, and I thought it looked like he was running in three directions at once. I didn't dare laugh.

It would be hard to say goodbye to my dear friend Clyde. I was going to miss him. No one could have been kinder or more caring than he was. His work ethic and positive attitude had me headed in the right direction.

I had worked all summer with only one minor injury, a cut on my right shin. My body was lean and hard, and I had actually gained some weight. I had lived and

North Idaho Junior College ca. 1955. Museum of North Idaho photo.

worked with an element of society that, at first glance, appeared to be mighty rough. But they were, really, mostly a collection of hardworking, caring, considerate, fun-loving men.

Without a doubt, I had gained an education in many ways. Most importantly, I had grown up. The boy was gone—the man had arrived.

Summer was over and it was time to move on. I would soon enroll as a full-time student at North Idaho Junior College.

Epilogue

I had no idea where this book-writing project would lead us. Our research uncovered volumes of unknown facts about my families. Although there are still unanswered questions, we have a mound of information about where they lived and worked with knowledge of their accomplishments as they survived the bad times and enjoyed the good times.

Today the long-ago homesteads are a study in contrasts. The Stowe property is crisscrossed with paved streets and has a house built on almost every one of its city lots. Interstate 90 cuts diagonally across the homestead and the constant roar of traffic and everyday living noises have replaced the peace and quiet of my great-grandfather's days.

My Grandfather Stowe's orchard property on the hill above Silver Beach has been developed as view property and those 160 $1 and $2 acres are now selling for an average of $450,000 an acre. Multi-million dollar homes are being built in that beautiful old orchard.

The Strobel homestead on the river, however, is completely uninhabited. The silence is only interrupted by the sounds of birds, the wind, and the faint sounds of traffic across the Valley on State Highway 3. The railroad track is no more, and the sounds of passing trains are gone forever; no steamboats on the river and no mill whistles at Lane.

Nature has reclaimed most of the land disturbed by mining activity near Killarney Lake, and only a handful of people reside in this area once well-populated with a series of small farms and ranches. The Strobel mine tunnel is still there, waiting patiently for miners who never appear. Were George and Celestia Strobel, along with their many relatives and friends, correct in their belief that extensive mineral wealth was hiding in their mountain? After years of thoughtful consideration my answer can only be "yes." I will never know for certain, but perhaps future generations will go exploring there again with modern techniques and equipment.

I do know it has been my extreme good fortune to have ancestors who made the decision to leave their established homes and farms and move west to settle in North Idaho. It has been a privilege to grow up and live my life in such a beautiful place. I stand in admiration of these people who exemplified the highest compliment in those bygone days—"He or she is a hard worker."

Numerous sawmills, the lifeblood of our area, are gone. The DeArmond Stud Mill, located on the edge of the Spokane River next to North Idaho College, was the last to go in the fall of 2008. Each closure was akin to the death of an old friend; the dismantling process a prolonged funeral and grieving period. The sad end of an era and a way of life is complete. The mill whistle blows no more.

Index